the Brownie Annual 1986

edited by
Rosalind Woodhouse

This annual belongs to . . .

£3.25

The Otter Trust

by Penny Morris

photographs by Tony Rose

Any of you who have been lucky enough to see an otter will know what delightful creatures they are, but nowadays the chances of your ever seeing an otter in the wild are very remote.

Over the last twenty years the number of otters in Europe has dropped rapidly, and now the situation is so serious that the otter is in danger of becoming extinct.

Since January 1st 1978 the British otter has been protected by law under the Conservation of Wild Creatures and Wild Plants Act 1975, making it illegal to hunt or kill an otter or disturb its resting place. But this is not enough.

The main threat to the survival of the otter is pollution. Otters spend much of their time in water, and rivers and waterways are essential to their survival. But our waterways are being polluted by poisons and chemicals from farming and industry, and the fish and frogs that the otters feed upon àre poisoned.

Another reason for the decline in the otter population is the destruction of their habitat; marshes are being drained, and riverbanks, which the otters use for their homes, are being straightened and neatened.

The Otter Trust was established to try and set up an otter haven where otters could live and breed in safety, with the ultimate intention of releasing groups of otters back into wild areas where a safe and suitable habitat remains.

The Otter Trust is open to the public and I went there with a group of local Brownies to see the otters in natural surroundings on the 23-acre site. The land includes three lakes, and a small stream flowing through the otters' breeding enclosures. As well as the otters, there are also many water fowl.

The cost of running the site is high and you can help support the Trust by becoming a member. For a small fee you get free admission to the Trust and regular newsletters informing you of the work of the Trust. If you are interested in finding out more about the Otter Trust, you can write to them at: The Otter Trust, Earsham, Near Bungay, Suffolk, NR35 2AF. Please enclose a stamped addressed envelope.

THE OTTER TRUST'S GROUNDS
YOU ARE HERE
Telephone Bungay 3470

Our Christmas Show

by Howard Tennant

illustrated by Shelagh McGee

Just imagine someone dressed in a pair of odd wellies, six sizes too big, their dad's old gardening jumper, and a big floppy hat belonging to their aunty Agnes; that's a typical costume for my friend Adele Boardman when she's doing one of her shows. I don't know! She says we're all daft at our house because we've so many pets, but they're just as potty in her house. I mean you can't blame Adele for being stage struck when you see the rest of her family.

Her dad is in Clayton Choral Union. They meet twice a week in the same place where we have our Brownie meetings. It's an old school that's massive. You should hear Adele's dad. He's always singing; it's usually stuff by a couple of men called Gilbert and Sullivan. He always makes me laugh when he's singing, especially when he sings the one about some Chinese women; it starts with "Three little maids from school," and Adele's dad squints his eyes and shuffles round with his arms folded.

Her mum pretends that she's not like the rest of the family, but last year we went to see her in the pantomime that the hospital put on at Clayton Community Centre. It was *Jack and the Beanstalk*. She played Jack's mother. She was great, especially the bit where she chased Jack with a rolling pin, and ended up falling into the laundry basket with her legs sticking up into the air. She was always telling Adele and her brothers not to act daft, but I know secretly she'd love to be joining in.

Adele's older brothers, Wayne and Karl, are in a pop group. Wayne plays the guitar and Karl is the drummer. They're both nuts. One night we were sitting in their kitchen when they both walked in. Without saying a word, Wayne started doing his Elvis Presley impression:

"It's one for the money, two for the show,
Three to get ready, now go cat go,
But don't you step on my blue suede shoes."

Karl started playing the drums first of all on the kettle and then on his dad's bald head!

Like I said, it's no wonder Adele is stage struck. One day at school, when we were doing art, Miss Finster, our teacher, suddenly put her finger on her lips for everyone to keep quiet. Adele was in the corner of the room looking at a reflection of herself in the glass door of one of the cupboards. She was doing one of the routines that she'd learnt at tap-dancing classes. She goes every Saturday without fail. Well, soon the whole class was quiet, watching Adele doing her routine. She was concentrating so hard she didn't notice we were watching. When she finished, Miss Finster clapped and one or two of the boys whistled, and do you know what? Adele didn't even go red. She just turned round, curtseyed very slowly, and then carried on washing out the paint pots.

You can imagine what she was like when, about a month before Christmas, Brown Owl announced that we were going to put on a little

Christmas Show to raise some money for the NSPCC. Brown Owl asked whether anyone had any ideas about what they could do in the show. Did anyone have any ideas! Do you know, every time you go past the Boardmans' garage, Adele is giving a show. Sometimes she has some of the children who live down their street watching and if she can't persuade them to come, she sits all her dolls and teddies on the floor and gives a show for them. She dances, she tells jokes (well, joke really, because she only knows one), she does magic tricks (from an old magic set Karl gave her), and she sings. She's got a good strong voice. My dad says that if ever they need a fog-horn on the Manchester Ship Canal, she would get the job easily. I know that's a bit unfair, but he said it after Adele had come looking for me up near where my dad keeps his pigeons, and when she shouted, "Janice!" at the top of her voice, it took my dad fifteen minutes to calm the pigeons down again.

"Mrs Colvin, Mrs Colvin, I've got some ideas," said Adele. All the other Brownies know what Adele is like, and one or two of them told Brown Owl how good she is.

"She's brill, Mrs Colvin," said Barbara Toland. "Honest, she's always giving shows in their garage."

"Yeah, she is," Paula Denny added. "My mum says she's a born performer."

"Well," said Mrs Colvin, "it looks as if you and I, Adele, are going to be the ones organising our show. Do you think we can do it before Christmas? There's not much time."

Brown Owl needn't have worried. She and Adele decided that the performance would be in two parts. The first half would be singing and dancing and so on, and then there would be a tea-break. After the break we would present a play about the animals who were in Bethlehem when Jesus was born. I was playing the part of one of the shepherds' dogs. It was quite easy really. All I did was pretend I was Sam, my dad's dog.

There were three different acts in the first part of the show; there was The Kids from Fame (Barbara Toland, Tracy Wilson, Deb Senior and Adele), then Miss Amazing and her Assistants, (Adele, and Cathy and Sandra Belton), and then Your Favourite TV Characters (Julie Dyson, Tabatha Simons, Julie Franks, and you-know-who). The rest of us were in the play, and some of us were going to work towards our Hostess Badge and help with the tea and look after our special guests (we'd invited the District Commissioner and the Vicar).

I was pretty busy learning my part in the play, so it wasn't until a few days before the actual Christmas Show that I had the chance to see what the first half was like. The Kids from Fame, as you might guess, were dancing and singing three songs from *Fame*. Adele has all the records and knows most of the dances as well. They looked and sounded quite good, and I asked Adele how she thought they were doing.

"For amateurs, not bad," she said. "But I'm a bit worried about Barbara's sense of rhythm."

"She looked all right to me," I said.

"Well, we'll soon know, won't we," she said in a thoughtful way.

Adele was on next, doing her magic tricks. She was really good, and Cathy and Sandra waved their arms all over the place just like magician's assistants do on the telly.

Last of all were the TV characters. Julie Dyson was Hilda Ogden, Tabatha Simons was Floella Benjamin from *Play Away*, Julie Franks was Morph, and Adele was Jimmy from The Krankies.

Everything went well at the dress rehearsal

on Thursday night, and we were all really excited at school on Friday thinking about the show. We all had to be at the school by six o'clock, and Mrs Colvin heaved a sigh of relief at quarter past, when Barbara Toland arrived, puffing and panting.

"I'm sorry I'm late, Mrs Colvin, but there was a big queue at the chippy, and Colin had to put some more fish in."

"Don't worry, Barbara, there's plenty of time to get into your leotard, and put on your knee warmers," Mrs Colvin replied.

"She means your purple leg warmers," Adele whispered to Barbara. "She's got a lot on her mind."

By five to seven the hall was packed. Adele and I peeped through the curtains and I waved to my mum and dad. I think my mum waved back, but I'm not sure. I think half of Clayton must've been in that hall, because there weren't enough chairs. Wayne and Karl said afterwards that they'd had to stand at the back.

Anyway, bang on seven o'clock, the curtains opened, the music started, and Clayton's answer to the New York School for the Performing Arts danced onto the stage. Adele was really good, and she got the others leaping and bouncing round the stage like nobody's business. The only problem came as they were doing the last dance. By that time, Barbara had stopped being nervous and as she was dancing she was busy looking for her mum and dad in the audience. She forgot that we only had a small stage, and went leaping too close to the edge. She was just about to do a cartwheel that would have ended with her doing a dive into the piano, when Adele took a firm grip on the back of her leotard and swung her round to face the back of the stage. Barbara's arms were going like a windmill, and as Adele let go, she executed a perfect cartwheel. The audience applauded loudly. They were sure it was all part of the act.

Adele dashed off stage when they finished and as Mrs Colvin was playing *The Sorcerer's Apprentice* on the piano, she jumped into her magician's outfit and dashed back on stage again with Cathy and Sandra, trying to look as elegant as you can when you're chasing after someone. Adele did really well. Paul Daniels couldn't have done better. At the end of the act she made my sister's guinea pig, Clapton, go from underneath one hat to another. At least,

that was the idea. She lifted the second hat up, but there was nothing there. Both Sandra and Cathy looked really worried. Adele apologised to the audience and said she hadn't done that trick before and she hoped they didn't mind it going wrong. You should have heard them. They all went, "Oh, never mind love," and, "Don't worry, pet," and, "What a shame," and were really sympathetic. Just then Adele noticed her mum in the front row of the audience, and went down the steps at the side of the stage, and up to her mum.

"She's really upset, isn't she?" whispered Barbara to me as we watched from the side of the stage, but just then Adele held up her mum's handbag for everyone to see, opened it, and took out Clapton! I thought the audience would never stop cheering. Adele ran back onto the stage, and as she and her assistants were coming off, Julie Dyson came on with a sweeping brush, doing her Hilda Ogden impression.

"Hello, chucks," she said. "They've given me time off from t'Rovers to come and sweep up after this lot." She looked great with her curlers and head scarf, and wandered around the stage singing in a high Hilda-ish voice.

Then Tabatha, who looks just like Floella Benjamin, came on to show her teddies how to dance like they do on *Fame*, and as she was doing that, Julie Franks, dressed in a long brown body-stocking and matching tights, moved onto the stage just like Morph does in *Take Hart*. Wayne said later that she looked just like a live sausage, and when you think about it, that's not a bad description of Morph!

Suddenly, from the back of the hall, a voice shouted, "Fan dabby dosy!" Everyone turned round to see who it was. Well, what a sight! Adele had her hair tucked up under her dad's old cricket cap; she had her old blazer on, a pair of Karl's old trousers cut to just above her knees, and her mum's wellies. She waddled up onto the stage and just stood there grinning a cheeky grin. She didn't need to say anything. The audience couldn't stop laughing. When they did calm down a bit Adele, who was standing with her legs wide apart, said, "I'm sorry that I'm walkin' a wee bit funny, but you see, I've got tadpoles in ma wellies, and I'm just takin' them for a walk," and with that she sploshed off stage.

After the interval we did our play about the animals, and except when Deb Senior's costume got caught on a nail and she couldn't move until I unhooked her, everything went smoothly. Brown Owl was really pleased. She was holding one guinea pig, and Adele held another (so that was how she did it!) while we all checked that we had everything to take home.

"Well, Brownies," she said, "that was terrific. You've all done marvellously to entertain so many people so well, and we've raised a considerable amount of money for the NSPCC. Well done, all of you."

"Perhaps we could do *Cinderella* at Easter?" Adele suggested.

Mrs Colvin looked at her, and just smiled.

GIRL GUIDES

Make an Owl Card

by Barbara Blease

To make your felt owl picture you will need:
brown felt 22 cm × 16 cm
yellow felt 10 cm square
paper for pattern, pins
Copydex or any good fabric glue
card for base

Trace all the shapes onto a piece of paper, including the large oval for the base, from the right side of the page. Cut out these pattern pieces from the paper. Lay the pattern pieces numbered 1, 2, 3, 4, 5 and 6 onto the brown felt, and pieces numbered 7, 8, 9, 10, 11 and 12 onto the yellow felt.

Pin all the pieces onto the felt and carefully cut around each one. Cut out the large oval base from the card. If the card is white or a piece of cereal box that is grey-coloured, paint or cover it before glueing on the felt. You are now ready to begin sticking down the felt pieces to make your felt owl picture. Glue the large brown piece numbered 1 onto the middle of the oval base. Have you remembered to cut out the spaces for the eyes, nose and feet?

All the other pieces of felt can now be glued in position on and around the owl, just like a jigsaw. Follow the numbers to find the correct position. When you glue on the nose, just stick down the top half of the diamond shape; this gives the owl a prominent nose.

When your owl picture is finished, make a loop of ribbon and glue it to the back of the card. Your owl is now ready to hang on the wall.

FOLK DANCING

GIRL GUIDES

by Valerie Nicholas

Dancing has been a way of showing our feelings since the day we were born. It is something we all enjoy doing whatever our age and whatever our taste in music. You must also remember that dancing is not just limited to those who go to ballet classes. It can be something that involves all of you.

Folk dancing is a particular form of dancing that involves a group of people. Perhaps your Brownie pack could get together and learn some of the social dances from other countries such as Austria, France, Greece, England or Scotland. They are fun to learn and you don't have to be a budding ballerina to be able to do the steps in these dances. To make it more interesting you could make a simple costume. A brightly coloured skirt with a white blouse also decorated with coloured braid would look quite stunning especially if everyone in the group had a different coloured skirt.

Here is a simplified English country dance for you to try with your pack. It can be performed to Bobby Shaftoe or any tune that has a similar beat to it. First of all divide your pack into groups of eight so that there are four couples in each group, and stand them in lines so that each group is separate from each other. Now you are ready to begin.

Every couple faces each other and holds hands at shoulder level. All moving in the same direction, everybody does four galops, and then everybody repeats the four galops in the opposite direction, returning to their original starting place.

Each couple now links right arms with their partners and does four skips round in their own little circle to return to their original position. Repeat this but link your left arms and turn your partner the other way.

The first couple of each group then hold hands at shoulder level and galop between the other couples so that they do four galops down to the bottom of their group and four galops back to their original position. The other couples in the group stand still and clap in time with the music until the first couple have finished their galops.

The first couple now drop hands and turn away from each other and skip down the outside of their group. The other couples follow. When the first couple reaches the position where the last couple has been standing, they stop and form a bridge with their arms. The other couples join hands and skip under the bridge with their partner and continue through so that the second couple now becomes the first couple. This can be repeated as many times as you wish.

Now let us turn to your scrapbook. There are lots of ideas and themes that can be used from a wide variety of

dance subjects such as ballet, tap, modern, national, ballroom, disco and gymnastic dance. Another way could be to discuss the different types of dancing seen on television and in the theatre or in dance companies. There could also be sections in your scrapbook about famous dancers, choreographers and different ballets and musicals. There are lots of interesting ways your scrapbook can be arranged so try and show your own particular interest in dance.

In the ballet stories section, most Brownies tend to think of well known ballets such as Swan Lake, Giselle, Coppelia, Cinderella or The Sleeping Beauty. But with a little bit of thought and research in your local library you could find out about not so well known ballets. Two books which you might find helpful are *Ballet Stories* by Joan Lawson and *Stories of the Ballets* by Gladys Davidson. Here are a few suggestions of ballets that might interest you.

The first is Anastasia, a dramatic ballet about Anna Anderson and her fight to be recognised as Anastasia, the youngest daughter of Tsar Nicholas II. The second ballet is the Graduation Ball, a story about the visit of young cadets to a girl's school for the graduation ball. And thirdly, the ballet Petrushka, set in Russia at a fair in St Petersburg in the 1830s, a story about a magician who has three puppets, Petrushka, a Ballerina and a Moor, and the love and hate between them, even after they have performed in public. Perhaps you will be able to find other ballet stories that interest you.

Another interesting section to chose is the one on national dancing where you have to know about the costumes, music and types of dancing seen in three countries. A very good book that will help you is *Folk Costumes of the World* by Robert Harrold, which has illustrations and descriptions of the many national costumes to be seen. Another book that will help you discuss the steps and music of European countries is *European Folk Dance* by Joan Lawson. Your local library will help you find these books.

Other ways of finding out about the national costumes of your chosen countries is by looking through travel brochures, or writing to the tourist office of a particular country or even by looking for postcards or buying the actual costume if you are lucky enough to go abroad for your holidays.

Whatever sections you choose in the Dancers Badge there is something for everyone, and the work you do will help increase your knowledge of dance.

Super Sunflowers!

by Jill Weekes

Brownies are cheerful people who like to keep busy all through the long winter months. So why not brighten up a dull February day by planting some little seeds that are full of summer sunshine?

A packet of sunflower seeds is well worth the money spent. Each stripey seed, approximately 1 centimetre in length, may grow, in the right surroundings, into a huge plant about 3 metres tall! Each leaf and yellow flower may measure more than 30 centimetres across.

People have always been fascinated by sunflowers, weaving stories and customs around them. An old legend tells that a water nymph, named Clytie, pined away and was changed into a sunflower, when Apollo, the sun god, did not return her love.

The South American Incas used sunflowers in their religious ceremonies. Sunflowers grew wild in South America, so the Inca craftsmen copied the flowerheads in wonderful designs of pure gold. Their golden sunflowers crowned and adorned the Virgins in the Inca Temple of the Sun. When Spanish soldiers landed in Peru in 1532, with their leader Francisco Pizarro, they were dazzled by the Inca gold, and were equally amazed by the giant, living sunflowers growing all around them.

The sunflower is not just good to look at, it is incredibly useful as well. An English collector of plants and herbs, called John Gerard, wrote in 1633 that sunflower buds could be "boiled and eaten with butter, vinegar and pepper, after the manner of artichokes".

North American Indians used to place bowls of sunflower seeds in the graves of dead warriors, in case they were hungry on the journey to the Happy Hunting Ground. This may seem a strange food to choose, but sunflower seeds are, in fact, very good for you. They are rich in Vitamin E, which keeps blood and muscles healthy.

Oil is extracted from the seeds nowadays, and used to make margarine, fats and sweets. Nothing is wasted, as the pulped seeds left over can be made into a 'cake', which is fed to cattle, sheep, pigs, poultry, pigeons and rabbits. Sunflower seed kernels can also be ground into flour, baked whole in cakes, sprinkled on salads, or roasted and used for coffee.

Sunflower leaves can be fed to animals, the stalks can be burnt for fuel, and the remaining ash dug back into the ground. The ash is rich in potash, a chemical which fertilizes the soil.

Bees love sunflowers, and make large amounts of honey and wax from them. We should love them too, as they are surely one of the earth's richest blessings.

If you plant sunflower seeds in pots indoors in February, transfer them to the garden in March or April. Otherwise, sow the seeds in March or April in a sunny position outdoors. Plant two or three seeds together, and later thin out the seedlings.

Perhaps you could have a sunflower race, to see which one grows tallest. It is great fun watching and measuring them — and collecting the seeds to dry and plant again the next year. You will have more than enough, so give some as Christmas or birthday presents, and spread a little sunshine through the gardens of your friends!

illustrated by Angela Beard

Brownies Round the World

by Debbi Scholes

illustrated by Chris Rothero

Belgium

As Belgium is a country which has two different languages, there is more than one kind of Brownie Pack. French speaking girls can belong to the Guides Catholiques, in which case they are called Lutin, or to the Federation des Eclaireurs et Eclaireuses, which is for both boys and girls, in which case they would be called a Louveteau, or Cub.

Those children who speak Flemish can join the Federatie voor open Scoutisme, which is also for boys and girls, or the Vlaams Verbond van de Katholieke Meisjesgidsen, which is just for girls. Those girls who join the VVKM would be called Kabouter.

A girl who is a Lutin makes this Promise: "With the help of the Lord Jesus, I promise to do my best to live according to the Brownie law." The Lutin Law is:

"The Brownie thinks first of others.
The Brownie learns to give pleasure.
The Brownie is joyful.
The Brownie tells the truth."

The Kabouter Promise is quite different: "I would like to live with the Brownies of the flower-house and will do my best to be a good Brownie." The Kabouter Law is:

"A Brownie knows how to listen (obey).
A Brownie is cheerful.
A Brownie joins in the games.
A Brownie enjoys giving pleasure."

As there are two languages in Belgium many of the road signs and place names, and even some shop signs, are written in both languages. This can make it difficult for foreigners to find their way around, as the two languages are very different. For instance the town which is called Le Coq in French is called De Haan in Flemish.

Belgium is very famous for chocolates, which are delicious. When you're in Belgium it doesn't make sense to buy an ordinary box of chocolates from a supermarket, when you can choose the exact flavours you want from a huge selection in a special chocolate shop. So if you only like hard centres you can choose only nutty ones!

Belgium is also famous for lace. On many street corners in Belgium you may see little old ladies sitting outside their doors engrossed in the intricate art of lace-making. At one time most Belgian girls were taught the art of lace-making, but nowadays young girls find it rather dull, and bad for their eyes, so the tradition is dying out. Even so, many shop windows are filled with delicate tablecloths, hankies and collars, all made in very fine lace.

As a large part of Belgium is very flat, rather like Holland, a favourite sport is cycling. Many Belgians belong to cycling clubs and take part in races. Whole families sometimes go on cycling holidays together.

The school hours in Belgium are similar to those in Britain but Belgian children generally have much more homework to do in the evenings. They have only a short holiday at Christmas and Easter, and a long, two month holiday in the summer. Most Belgian school children have their midday meal at home, as for most families, lunch is the main meal of the day, when the whole family sits down together.

Food is very important in Belgium and as no area is very far from the sea, fish is very popular. Chips, or pommes frites, are also a great favourite with Belgians, especially eaten with mayonnaise, and you can find stalls selling 'frites' on street corners all over the country. Many stalls also sell hot waffles, which are absolutely delicious.

Photograph reproduced by kind permission of the Mexican Government Tourist Office

Mexico

A Mexican Brownie is called a Hadita. She does a Good Turn by being helpful at home, looking after her brothers and sisters, and keeping herself neat and tidy. Many Haditas also go to visit the children in local orphanages, playing with them, teaching them games, and helping them to make toys and clothes.

Mexico, as I expect most of you know, is situated south of the United States of America. It is over twenty times larger than the United Kingdom, but the population is about the same. Most people in Mexico speak Spanish as many years ago, Spanish people invaded Mexico searching for gold, jewels, and other treasures that they believed could be found there. Not everyone speaks Spanish, however; there are also many Indian tribes who speak their own languages.

Mexico is quite a poor country and many children find jobs to help earn extra money for their families when they are only seven or eight years old. They wash cars, clean shoes, or catch fish and sell them on the beaches, just to earn a few pesos, the currency used in Mexico.

Mexican Brownies make the following Promise:

"Yo prometo hacer cuanto de mi
dependa para cumplir con mi deber
hacia Dios y mi Patria, ayudar a
todos, todos los dias, especialmente
a los de mi case."

"I promise to do my best to do my
duty towards God and my country,
and to help everyone each day,
especially those of my own home."

The Mexican Brownie Motto is *Dar Ayuda*, which means Help Others.

A very popular dish in Mexico, which you could use as a dip at parties, is Guacamole. The ingredients you need to make it are: two ripe avocado pears, two tablespoons lemon juice, two cloves garlic, a teaspoon chilli powder, and a little salt. To prepare it, cut the avocados in half, watching out for the stone in the middle. Remove the outer skin and the stones (keep them if you want to try growing an avocado plant), then scrape all the flesh into a bowl, making sure you get all the dark green flesh that is close to the skin. Peel and crush the garlic, and put it into the bowl with the avocados, and all the other ingredients. Mash up the avocados and mix all the ingredients together until the mixture is smooth and creamy. You can add a little mayonnaise if you want to make it more creamy. Serve it in a pretty bowl, with raw vegetables such as celery and carrots to dip into it, or you can use savoury biscuits if you prefer.

Every town in Mexico has a fiesta day, the most important day of the year for many people. As the word suggests, this is a festival, usually to commemorate a particular saint. Many festivals are also held during the first six days of January, and on the sixth day Mexican people exchange gifts. They do this in celebration of the presents given to baby Jesus by the three Kings. It is called the day of the Three Wise Men, and traditionally Mexican children receive gifts left in their shoes, rather than having things left in their stockings on Christmas Day as we do. Many families hold a big party on this day, and a cake is baked filled with small tokens made of porcelain. One of the tokens is a tiny doll, and whoever gets that token in their piece of cake has to give a party in February for the whole family, to mark the end of the festivities. Eating the cake is quite difficult as porcelain is very hard; a careless bite could result in a visit to the dentist!

Pakistan

Brownies in Pakistan are called Junior Guides although they do much the same sort of activities as you. Some Packs wear long white shifts with white trousers underneath and a coloured sash over the shoulder and crossing at the front. They sew their badges on these.

At one time Pakistan was part of India but when India became independent in 1948 the people who were Muslims decided that they wanted to be a separate country from India, so Pakistan was created. Unfortunately, the areas where the Muslims lived were far apart so originally Pakistan was divided into two parts, East Pakistan and West Pakistan, but now the area that was formerly called East Pakistan is called Bangladesh, so West Pakistan is just called Pakistan now.

Many people in Pakistan villages live in houses made of hardened clay or mud bricks. The houses are quite small and have very little furniture. Many families grow their own food. The climate is too hot and dry to grow rice, so most families have fields where they grow wheat, which is used to make chapatis, which are like thin pancakes. They only eat rice on special occasions. The chapatis are used to pick up food instead of using a utensil. If you get the chance to eat in a Pakistani restaurant in the UK ask if you can have chapatis instead of rice, and try eating your curry with them. It's not as messy as it sounds!

In the schools in Pakistan the children study much the same subjects as you. As well as history, geography and arithmetic, most school children learn English, too, as it is considered an important language in Pakistan. Many newspapers and magazines are written in English, and sometimes Pakistani people from different areas speak to each other in English as their own languages are so different. In the Punjab area of Pakistan the children speak Punjabi, but usually write in Urdu. Urdu writing uses many curves and squiggles, so the children have to use special pens made from reeds.

Many Pakistani children enjoy flying kites as a hobby, and sometimes they have kite flying competitions. The kite strings are covered with glue and sprinkled with ground glass, then the children try to cut each other's strings as they steer their own kite across the strings of the opponent's kite. Sport is also popular in Pakistan, the favourite sports being cricket, hockey, squash and soccer.

A typical dish from Pakistan is Pilau Rice. To make enough for three or four people you need: 225g/8oz long grain rice, 3tbsp cooking oil, salt and pepper, and 1 litre/2 pints of boiling water or chicken stock. First heat the oil in a large, heavy-bottomed pan, and when it is hot add the rice and fry it gently, stirring it all the time. Add salt and pepper and when the grains of rice become translucent or see-through, slowly add the liquid, taking care not to splash. When you have added all the liquid, stir the rice, then put a lid on the pan and cook it over a very low heat for about 15 minutes, until the rice has absorbed all the liquid. Serve this rice with a curry or as a change from potatoes with any other dish. If you want to make it more interesting, add a handful of sultanas, slivers of almond, and some chopped, hard-boiled egg.

Know Your Birthstone

by Jill Weekes illustrated by Dee McLean

Of course, you know your birthday, you almost certainly know your birth sign, but how well do you know the birthstone for your month? Read on, and impress your friends and family with your amazing knowledge!

JANUARY: Garnet

The best known garnets are a beautiful, glowing red, though brown and green ones are also found in South Africa, Australia and North America. The garnet is formed from crystallized minerals. Its name probably comes from the Latin word *granatum*, meaning pomegranate: perhaps the Romans thought garnets looked like pomegranate seeds!

According to legend, Noah brought light to the whole Ark, during the dark days of the Great Flood, with a single fiery garnet.

The Ancient Egyptians loved the garnet's vivid colour, and in Ancient India and Persia, a bracelet of garnets was said to protect the wearer from poison, plague and lightning!

During the Middle Ages in Europe, the garnet was thought to have the power to cure high fever.

The January garnet is said to symbolize faithfulness, power and friendship. If it is your stone, the outlook is good for you!

FEBRUARY: Amethyst

The amethyst, a variety of purple quartz, is found in the USSR and South America. Its name, from the Greek word *amethystos*, means *not drunk*. Long ago, drinking cups set with amethysts were thought to charm away drunkenness!

Ancient Egyptian and Greek princesses wore wonderful amethyst necklaces. Roman ladies thought the amethyst would protect their husbands, and keep them faithful. It was said to be St Valentine's favourite stone: his amethyst ring was engraved with a cupid (the god of love). Thus, the amethyst became a popular stone with sweethearts.

The amethyst was thought for centuries to inspire duty and devotion. For this reason, it was worn by bishops in their rings. It was also a royal stone: the first English king to wear the amethyst as a royal emblem was Edward the Confessor in the 11th century.

The amethyst, today, represents sincerity and authority. If your birthday is in February, perhaps you possess these qualities?

MARCH: Aquamarine

The blue or blue-green aquamarine is a variety of a mineral called beryl, and is found in the USSR and Brazil. Its name is a Latin word meaning *sea water*: the Romans, long ago, carved aquamarines into the shapes of sea gods.

For centuries, the aquamarine was regarded as a lucky stone. Worn in a bracelet, it was thought to prevent harm and accident, or in difficult times to bring comfort and reassurance. It was also said to keep its wearer looking young! During the Middle Ages, fortune tellers used the aquamarine as a form of crystal ball for predicting the future.

Today, the aquamarine is supposed to bring March birthdays the gifts of courage, happiness and long-lasting love!

APRIL: Diamond

The diamond, formed of pure crystallized carbon, the hardest natural substance, is mined in Brazil, the USSR and South Africa.

Found in many colours from white to green and brown, its name comes from the Greek word *adamas*, meaning unconquerable. Perhaps it is called this because, as it is so hard, it can be cut or polished only by another diamond.

During the Middle Ages, diamonds were thought to protect the wearer from plague. Queen Elizabeth I, in the 16th century, wore a diamond to guard her from infection.

The diamond was said to ward off evil, especially when worn on the left side. This may be the reason it was chosen for engagement rings. Maximillian of Hapsburg gave the first recorded diamond engagement ring to Mary of Burgundy in 1477.

The April diamond represents

innocence, purity and happiness in marriage: perhaps you will wear it one day!

MAY: Emerald

The rich, green emerald, a variety of the mineral beryl, is found in South America, South Africa and the USSR.

Long ago, it was dedicated to Venus, the goddess of love, and said to be her favourite stone.

The emerald was thought to help poor eyesight: the Roman Emperor Nero, who had weak eyes, used a sliced emerald to enable him to see the gladiators in the arena. Perhaps this old belief explains why green is said to be the most restful colour for eyes.

Sailors once wore uncut emeralds round their necks, with the rough side against the skin, as a protection against drowning. The emerald was also used to ward off evil spirits, fits and stomach infections.

In the 18th century, a poet named William Drennan called Ireland 'the Emerald Isle', because of its green landscape; this name has never been forgotten.

The emerald stands for love and success, happy prospects for those with birthdays in May.

JUNE: Pearl

For centuries, pearls were a mystery. The early Greeks knew they were found in oysters: *margarite*, an old name for pearls, comes from *margaritafera*, the Greek word for oyster. (It has given us the English name Margaret). Why pearls appeared in oysters, though, no one knew for certain.

The Romans believed pearls were formed from raindrops, which fell into the open oyster shells, then hardened. The early Christians thought them to be angels' tears, shed for the sins of mankind and preserved in the sea.

Pearls are, in fact, made by the oysters themselves. When a speck of sand or grit irritates the

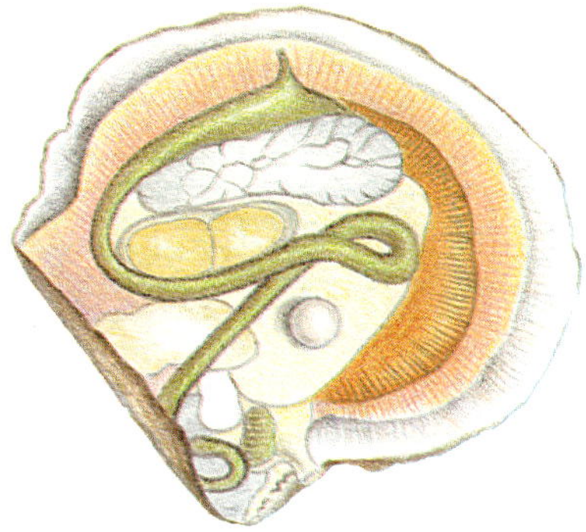

oyster, the creature surrounds it with nacre, the shiny substance which lines its shell. The pearls it thus produces may be creamy white, pink, yellow, grey or even black. They are harvested today mainly in the Persian Gulf and off the Australian coast.

Pearls have always been highly valued: the Roman Emperor Julius Caesar ruled that only ladies of high rank should wear them.

The pearl is said, nowadays, to represent beauty, health and innocence. The outlook is good for June!

JULY: Ruby

The ruby, found in India and Ceylon, is a red variety of a mineral called corundum. The Ancient Hindus believed it to possess inner heat, and thought a ruby placed in water would make it start boiling!

Rubies were worn in the Middle Ages to protect the wearer from drowning and rheumatic pain. They could, it was believed, cure plague, poisoning and sorrow, and keep the mind free from evil.

The 13th century explorer, Marco Polo, described how the King of Ceylon owned a ruby as long as a man's hand and as thick as his arm. The king would not part with it, even though the Emperor of China offered a city for it.

Rubies have always been favourites with royalty, often chosen for Coronation rings. A magnificent ruby appears in the English State Crown, kept in the Tower of London.

The ruby is said to symbolize contentment, love and devotion: a very happy stone!

AUGUST: Peridot

The peridot is a transparent green variety of a mineral called olivine, and is found in Burma and Thailand. No one knows how it got its strange name, although the *Peri*, a fairy in old Persian legends, who helped pure souls reach heaven, may have had something to do with it!

The peridot was thought to bring powers of great bravery to its wearer.

Soldiers who journeyed to the Crusades in the 11th and 12th centuries, treasured peridots as they also believed that the stones kept their loved ones faithful.

Peridots were very popular with early 19th century English ladies, who wore them in rings and earrings. A Victorian designer used a peridot for the body of a jewelled housefly – its wings were made of diamonds.

The girl born in August should definitely make a good wife: the peridot symbolizes happiness in marriage, peace of mind, and trust!

SEPTEMBER: Sapphire

The clear blue sapphire, belonging to the mineral family corundum, is mined in Burma and Thailand. Green, pink, orange and yellow sapphires are also occasionally found.

The Ancient Persians thought that the earth rested on a giant sapphire, whose blue reflection was seen in the sky.

As it mirrored the blue of heaven, the sapphire was for a long time regarded as a holy stone. A Pope in the 6th century instructed church cardinals to wear a sapphire on the right hand when making the blessing.

A sapphire was said to protect its owner from captivity, bring peace between enemies, and charm away evil spirits. Scorcerers used sapphires to help them predict the future.

The sapphire brings great gifts to the September girl: clear thinking, charm and enduring love!

OCTOBER: Opal

The opal belongs to the mineral family silica, and is found in many colours in Australia and South America. The most familiar opal is milky white, and flashes rainbow colours. The early Romans believed the opal brought good luck, and regarded the 'rainbow' in the stone as a sign of hope.

For a long time, the opal was thought to give protection against poisoned food: noblemen usually carried one, as poisoning used to be common. The opal was also said to have the power of making the wearer invisible to his enemies. Perhaps this was wishful thinking!

Blonde ladies in the Middle Ages thought that wearing an opal necklace would prevent their hair from turning darker.

Touching the forehead with an opal was said to give a good memory!

The opal was the favourite stone of Queen Victoria. There is a collection of royal jewels which includes opals carved in the shapes of a bird, cat, fish and dog.

October opals bring hope, faith and good fortune to their birthday girls: very lucky stones!

NOVEMBER: Topaz

Topaz is a yellow mineral crystal, though it is occasionally found in brown, pink or blue in Australia, the USSR and the Americas. It may take its name from *tapas*, an old word meaning fire.

Like many stones, the topaz was said to have great powers. The Roman Emperor Hadrian was the proud owner of an ancient topaz ring, inscribed with a prophecy of good luck. The stone was thought to prevent fits and asthma, and an unusual cure for sleeplessness was a drink made from water in which a topaz had been soaked!

During the Middle Ages, the topaz was believed to chill a bowl of boiling water when placed inside it – unlike the ruby, which was supposed to make water boil.

Eighteenth century English ladies loved to wear collar-shaped necklaces, hung with topaz pendants. The Victorians admired topaz stones too, and set them in leaf and flower shapes.

The topaz brings the November girl faithfulness, true friendship and loyalty: she should be in great demand!

DECEMBER: Turquoise

The blue-green turquoise, found in Iran, the USSR and the Americas, contains copper, aluminium and iron. It is thought to be one of the first stones ever mined, and was highly prized in Ancient Mexico and Egypt. Some gold serpent bracelets, set with turquoise, found in a Pharaoh's tomb, date from 3500 B C.

Long ago, the turquoise was known as *turkis* or *turkeystone*, because it was brought through Turkey on its way to Europe from Persia. The early Turks and Tibetans used the turquoise as a lucky charm, especially for horsemen. It was thought to prevent broken bones, by absorbing the crack if its owner fell off his horse! In 20th century Iran, camels, horses and mules still often have turquoise beads tied to their tails.

The Persians thought the magical blue of the turquoise would protect them from evil spirits. It was also known as a sweethearts' stone, which would keep rivals away and guarantee faithfulness.

The turquoise is said to bring fortunate December girls health, wealth and happiness. Who could ask for more?

Next time you pass a jeweller's, try and spot your stone. Could it bring you fame and fortune? Or would you need these first, before you could afford to buy it? Don't take the old tales too seriously, but get to know your birthstone – it can give you a lot of fun!

PUZZLES

WORD SQUARE

by Ann Hillyer

Solve these clues and then find the words in the square.

1. Try to do one every day (4–4).
2. This Six Emblem looks as if he has his House Orderly! (5).
3. You wear this to Brownies (7).
4. Christian name of the World Chief Guide (5).
5. Learn this to gain an Interest Badge (5–3).
6. Our Founder was Lord . . . (5–6).
7. The first Brownie Journey is along the . . . (8).
8. The shape of your Promise Badge (7).
9. F sharp is a . . . you may need to know for Musician Badge (4).
10. Small group of Brownies within a Pack (3).
11. The last of the Brownie Journeys (7).
12. I wonder if this Six is mischievous? (3)
13. Perhaps your Pack has one of these flying in their Ring (4).
14. The middle Brownie Journey (4).
15. You sew these Badges on your right arm (8).
16. This Six Emblem is blue (3).
17. Brownies help at . . . (4).
18. The Brownie Motto (4–1–4).
19. Brownies sit in this Ring to discuss secrets (3–3).
20. When you are a Guide you will learn to use them (4).
21. A group of Brownies is called a . . . (4).
22. Always do this at the kerb (4).
23. This Interest Badge has a saucepan on it (4).
24. Some Brownies look into this before making their Promise (4).

JUMBLED TOWNS

The station master's signs have all been jumbled up. Each line of letters needs to be rearranged to make an English town. When you have unjumbled them, place all the town names in a different order and you will find that the initial letters spell the name of an eighth town.

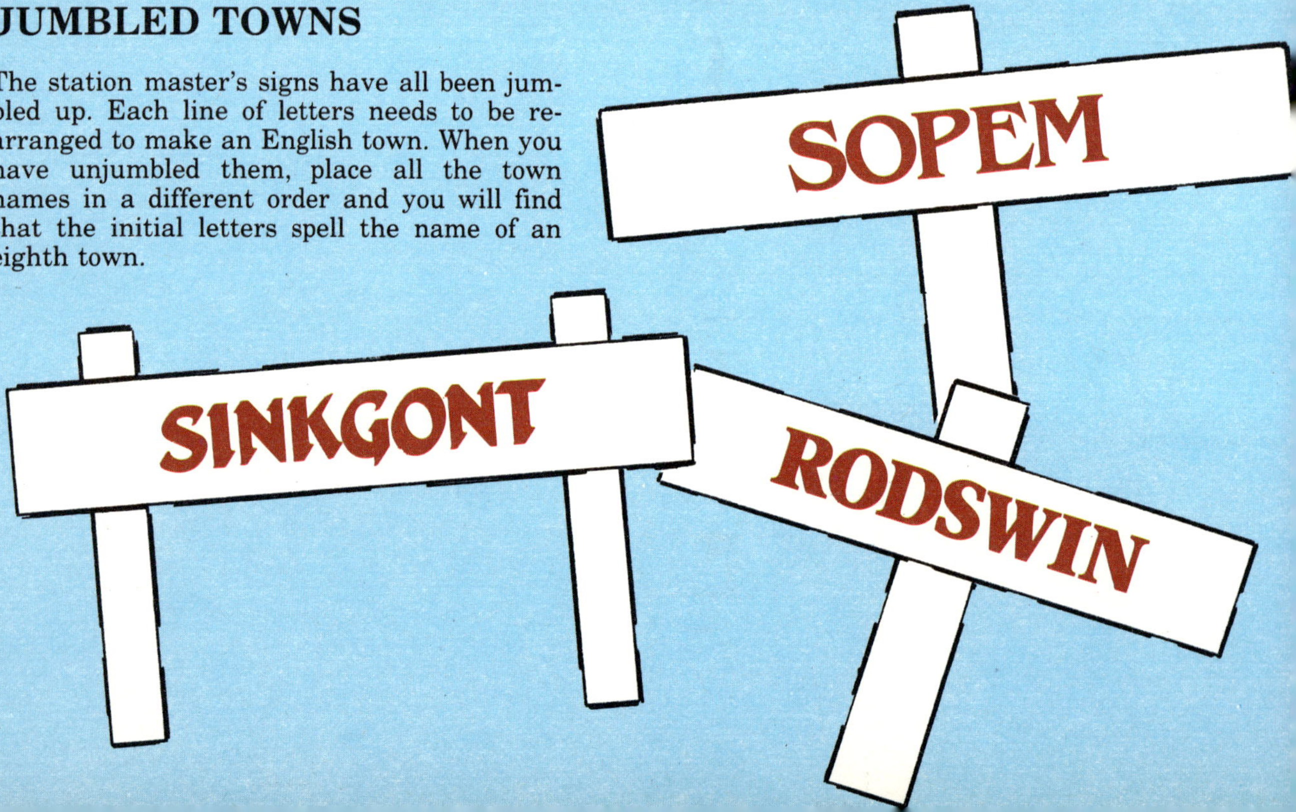

25. Could you make one of these to give to a child? (3).
26. For your Swimmer Badge you have to do one of these from a board, bank or boat (4).
27. This sort of tree grows from an acorn (3).
28. Brownies should have this out-of-doors (3).
29. When you are a Guide you may go to . . . (4).
30. For your Musician Badge you might choose to do this (4).
31. All First Aiders should be able to tie a reef . . . (4).
32. To gain this Interest Badge you might do this or crochet (4).
33. This is the leader of a Six (5).
34. One way to help at home is to make this every day (3).

U	I	R	P	M	A	C	Y	L	P	Z
G	N	O	M	E	U	X	O	O	A	R
O	T	I	I	K	N	I	T	O	C	E
O	E	L	F	N	Q	S	O	P	K	X
D	R	F	O	O	T	P	A	T	H	I
T	E	I	L	T	R	A	G	N	I	S
U	S	R	A	O	E	M	O	N	G	W
R	T	S	V	J	F	D	N	A	H	A
N	O	T	E	P	O	W	W	O	W	D
D	G	A	L	F	I	W	M	K	A	N
E	V	I	D	U	L	E	A	C	Y	E
B	A	D	E	N	P	O	W	E	L	L

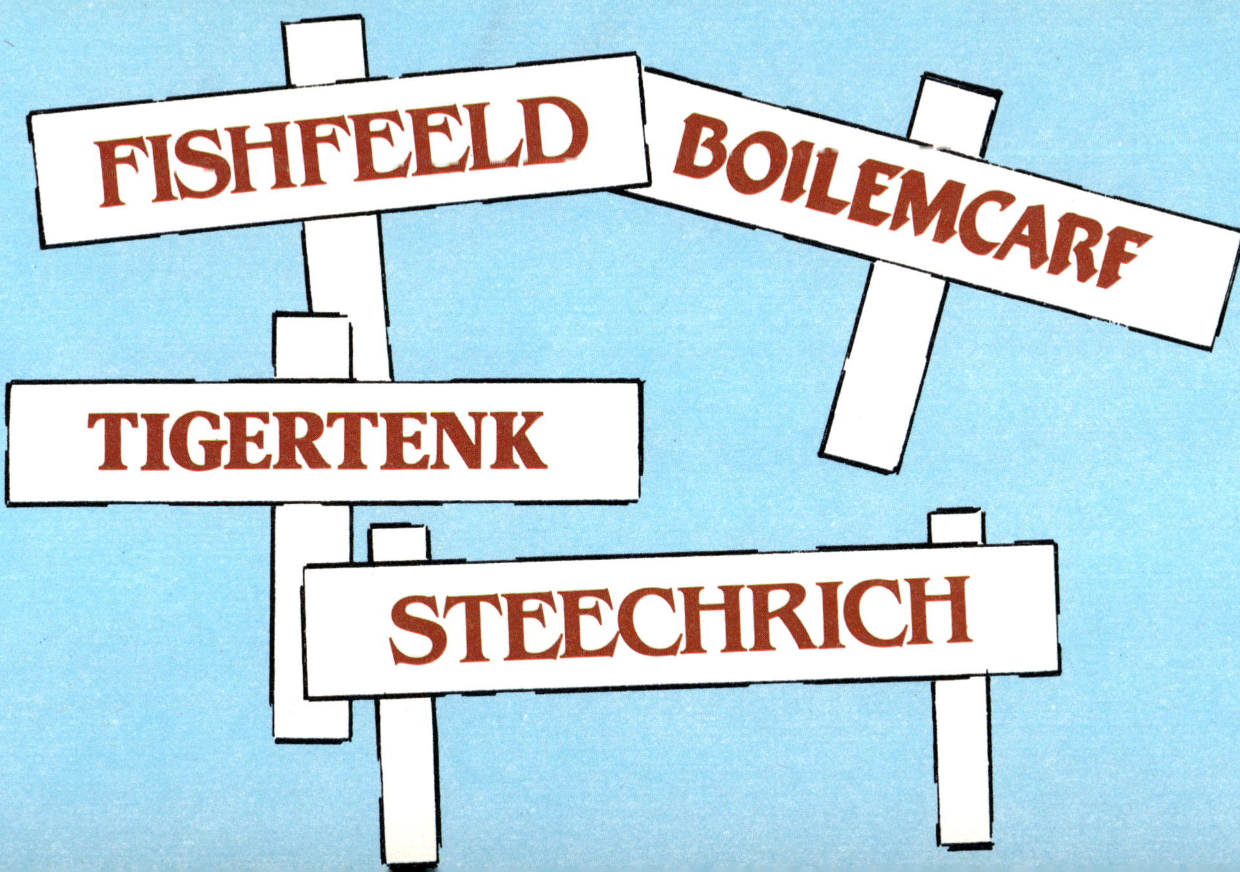

Hey, good cooking!

by Doreen Forni

illustrated by Jil Shipley

Nowadays the variety of fruit and vegetables that you can buy from supermarkets, shops and market stalls is enormous. They come from all over the world, and include the familiar oranges and lemons and the exotic mangoes and passion fruits. Besides being delicious to eat, and fun to cook, fruit and vegetables are very good for you, too.

VITAL VEG

Stuffed tomatoes

You can buy large tomatoes in most shops now and these are ideal for stuffing. Sometimes they are called 'beef' tomatoes. They are grown in Holland, Italy and other Mediterranean countries.

For four people you will need four large tomatoes. Wash them and place them stalk end down on a worktop. Cut a 'lid' off the top and carefully scoop out the flesh using a teaspoon, leaving the skin intact.

Put the flesh in a basin and mash it up.

There are many different fillings you can use to stuff tomatoes. Here are two suggestions:

1 Take two slices of bread (brown or white), remove the crusts, and make them into crumbs using a grater. Put into the basin with the tomato flesh. Add 2–3oz/50–75g grated cheese, cottage cheese or curd cheese. Add two slices of bacon, with the rind removed and cut into small pieces. Mix all the ingredients together, adding a pinch of salt and pepper.

2 Take two slices of bread, crumbed as above, and put them in the basin. Drain a small tin of tuna fish, and add the fish to the basin. Wash two or three small mushrooms, chop them up and add them to the basin. Mix all the ingredients together and add a pinch of salt and pepper.

When you have mixed your stuffing, put the tomato cases into an ovenproof dish and carefully fill them with the mixture. Replace the lids that you cut off, then put two tablespoons of water in the dish. Put the dish on a baking tray and put it in the oven. Cook them for 30–40 minutes, until they feel soft when pricked with a knife. Serve them with toast and a green salad.

Stuffed peppers

You can buy green, red, and sometimes white, yellow or purple peppers. Any of these are suitable for stuffing. Their real name is Capsicum, and they originated in South America, but are now grown in Mediterranean countries, particularly in Israel. They don't taste hot, but are slightly sweet, especially the red ones. They can be used raw in salads, but are also very tasty cooked with a savoury stuffing.

You need one pepper for each person. Cut off the top, scoop out the core and seeds and rinse them well under the tap. Put the peppers in a pan, cover them with water and bring it slowly to the boil. When it boils, cook the peppers gently for five minutes, then carefully drain them, and stand them in an ovenproof dish with two tablespoons of water in it.

You can use the same fillings as for the tomatoes, but you need to make a little more, as there is no tomato flesh.

Rice makes a good filling, but you must cook it first in boiling water. Mix it with chopped, grilled bacon, chopped mushrooms and sultanas, salt and pepper.

Put the stuffing into the pepper shells and put a small piece of butter or margarine on top of each. Cover the dish with a lid or a piece of tin foil, and cook in the oven at gas mark 4/180°C/350°F for 30–40 minutes. Serve as a supper dish.

Even the humble potato can taste special when made into individual cottage pies.

Cottage pies

Light the oven at gas mark 4/180°C/350°F. You need two large, even-sized potatoes for four people, 1 tin of minced beef with onions (or 12oz/325g mince cooked with onions), 1 tbsp tomato puree, 1oz/25g butter or margarine, and a little milk.

If the potatoes are very large, put them in a saucepan, cover them with cold water and bring them to the boil. Then carefully drain away the water, and put the potatoes in the oven. If they are medium sized potatoes put them straight in the oven, pricking them first to prevent them bursting. Bake them for 1–1½ hours until they feel soft right through.

While the potatoes are cooking, mix together the cooked mince and the tomato puree.

When the potatoes are done, take them out of the oven. Cut the potatoes in half and then, holding them with a cloth, as they will be very hot, scoop out the potato flesh into a bowl. Add the butter, milk, salt and pepper and mash it well together.

Put the potato skins into an ovenproof dish, divide the mince mixture between them, then put the mashed potato on top, covering the mince neatly.

Put the dish in the oven and heat through to brown the potato. Serve with a green vegetable.

DELIGHTFUL DESSERTS

Orange ice-ation

You need one orange per person, and one lemon and 2oz/50g sugar for every four oranges.

Cut the oranges into basket shapes as in the picture. You may need to ask an adult to help you do this. Scoop out all the flesh and pull away the pith and skin from the cut-out pieces. Cut all the flesh into small pieces on a plate so you don't lose the juice. Squeeze the juice from the lemon and mix it with the sugar. Pour this over the orange flesh, and put it back into the orange baskets. Put the baskets on a plate and pop it into the fridge to get cold.

Potato sandwiches

Instead of putting a burger into a bap or soft roll, serve it between two potato cakes.

For four people you need 2lbs/900g potatoes, and 2oz/50g flour.

Cook the potatoes in boiling water until they are soft then drain them, and mash them with the flour and a pinch of salt and pepper. Put the potato mixture onto a floured worktop, and very gently roll it out until it is about ½″/1cm thick. Cut out rounds using a cutter about 4″/10cm across. Repeat until you have eight rounds.

Gently fry the potato cakes in a little oil or lard, until they are lightly browned on both sides. Remove them from the pan and keep them hot on a plate in the oven.

For the burgers you need 8oz/200g raw minced beef, a grated onion, 1 slice of bread made into crumbs, 1 tablespoon of tomato ketchup, an egg, salt, pepper and a pinch of mixed herbs.

Mix all the ingredients together very well, using a fork, then flour your hands and divide the mixture into four, and shape into burgers. Fry them lightly on both sides in the same pan you used for the potato cakes. They will take about 20 minutes to cook right through. When they are done, remove them from the pan, and serve them between two potato cakes.

Baked bananas

You probably eat bananas raw usually, but why not try them cooked for a change?

You need two bananas for each person. Peel them and put them in an ovenproof dish.

In a small saucepan, put the juice of two oranges and 2oz/50g brown sugar. Heat it gently stirring with a wooden spoon, and when the sugar has melted, pour the syrup over the bananas. Put the dish into the oven at gas mark 4/180°C/350°F for 25 minutes.

Serve them hot with cream or ice cream. You could use lemon juice instead of orange, but you would need to add more sugar.

PUZZLES

BADGE SYMBOLS
by Suzanne Brown

A	S	A	U	W	O	A	D	I	S
M	A	G	N	I	F	Y	I	N	G
A	U	B	A	N	T	E	R	G	L
S	C	A	R	R	O	W	O	T	A
T	E	E	R	E	A	R	T	I	S
A	P	I	O	P	F	R	I	N	S
D	A	N	C	E	R	C	W	E	B
S	N	E	F	O	A	E	K	C	E
W	D	O	D	T	M	A	R	A	W
A	A	B	W	O	O	L	A	M	S

Which symbols are found on the following badges? Find the names of the symbols in the square above.

1. Swimmer
2. Conservation
3. Collector
4. Toymaker
5. Cook
6. Pathfinder
7. Knitter
8. Animal lover
9. Craft
10. Dancer

Spot the Herb
by Marion Kershaw

1. I have rough dry leaves.
   My flowers are mauve.
   You'll find me stuffed in a chicken.

2. I have delicate blue flowers.
   I am for remembrance.
   I have a pretty girl's name.

3. I have crisp curly leaves.
   I go well with sauce and fish.
   I am a character in a book.

4. I have long pointed leaves.
   Use me in jelly, vinegar and sauce.
   I can be sweet or savoury.

5. I like to keep warm.
   My name is a boy's.
   I am delicious in soup.

6. I am a small neat plant.
   I like to run over paths.
   It is said that rabbits make tea of me.

7. My leaves are grey-green.
   I may be Dutch or English.
   You can find me in bags.

8. I have pretty mauve or yellow flowers.
   My roots are more important.
   You'll find me in medicines and sweets.

WORK IT OUT! by Ann Hillyer

Sally and Lucy have been saving pennies in a jar to give to charity. Sally gives Lucy as many pennies as Lucy already has. Lucy then gives Sally as many pennies as Sally has left. They then find that Sally has 36p and Lucy has 42p. Can you work out how many pennies each girl had to start with?

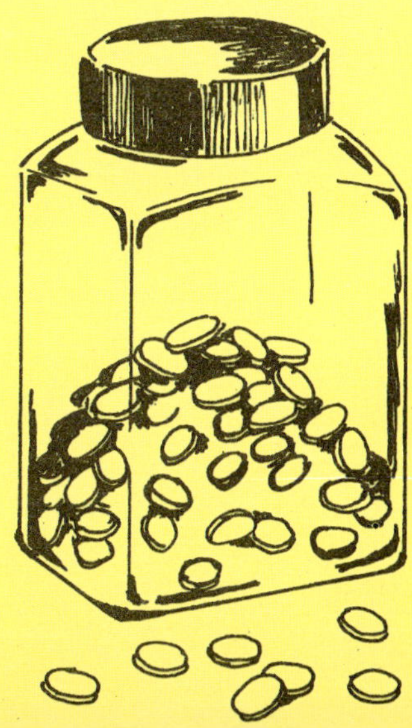

Answers on page 61.

MERRY MUSIC

by Hilda Young

The stories behind some nursery rhymes

An early lullaby

When the Pilgrim Fathers arrived on the shores of America to start a new life there, they saw and heard many strange sights. One young man was very surprised to see how an Indian mother carried her baby in a kind of bag on her back as she worked in the fields.

He was even more amazed to see another mother hang a birch-bark cradle high up in the treetops. As the wind blew, the cradle rocked gently in the breeze, lulling the baby to sleep, safe from the wild animals which roamed the woods and fields below.

The young Englishman returned to his own stockade and made up a little rhyme which mothers still sing as a lullaby today:

"Hush-a-bye, baby, on the tree top,
When the wind blows, the cradle will rock;
When the bough breaks, the cradle will fall;
Down will come baby, cradle and all!"

Two merry monarchs

Several centuries ago there lived in Reading, Berkshire, a clothier, a man who sold bales of cloth, named Colebrook. The business of Master Colebrook prospered, and because he was an extremely kindhearted man, he shared his great wealth with others less fortunate than himself. He also ensured that others found employment by finding work for over three hundred people. He was very fond of music, inviting wandering musicians to play for him and, having a merry sense of humour, he would often try to play their instruments himself.

Loved by all who knew him, he was called a 'king among men' for his many kindnesses, and a rhyme was written about him:

"Old King Cole
Was a merry old soul,
And a merry old soul was he;
He called for his pipe,
He called for his bowl,
And he called for his fiddlers three."

Another nursery rhyme monarch was the king who received a pie containing twenty-four blackbirds. Some people believe that this was a novelty dish to provide a sweet-singing surprise for Henry the Eighth. But more believe that it recalls the days when Henry seized all the monasteries and their treasures for himself: the Abbot of Glastonbury, eager to stay on good terms with the king, sent Henry the deeds of twenty-four fine manor houses hidden in a pie crust. But on the way the steward took one of the deeds out for himself, so Henry only received twenty-three 'blackbirds'. The steward, Master Horner, is remembered in two rhymes, the sing a song of sixpence ditty and the one about Jack who found a fine plum in his pie!

Oranges and lemons

Most of you will have played the popular singing nursery rhyme game of 'Oranges and Lemons' but have you ever wondered *why* the different bells sang out what they did?

St Clement's church is near where oranges and lemons were landed from the sunny Mediterranean countries. St Martin's, which is asking for the repayment of five farthings, is St Martin's Lane where the money lenders lived, and the Old Bailey was near the debtors' prison where those who did not pay their debts were sent. The bells of Shoreditch asked for time to pay, saying he would one day grow rich like Dick Whittington, who was told by the great bell of Bow to turn again and seek his fortune in the city of London. Dick followed the advice of the bells and became a prosperous merchant, rich enough to lend money to the king himself, and become Lord Mayor three times!

"Oranges and lemons
Say the bells of St Clement's.
You owe me five farthings,
Say the bells of St Martin's.
When will you pay me?
Say the bells of Old Bailey.
When I grow rich,
Say the bells of Shoreditch.
When will that be?
Say the bells of Stepney.
I'm sure I don't know,
Says the great bell of Bow."

Fur and feather music

Long ago country folk believed that on February 14th, St Valentine's Day, all the birds chose their mates. Cock Robin fell in love with Jenny Wren and, knowing she loved sweet music, sang to her until she finally consented to become his wife . . . as this rhyme shows. It is the first verse of a long poem telling of Robin's wooing and marriage to Jenny.

"Cock Robin got up early
At the break of day,
And went to Jenny's window
To sing a roundelay.
He sang Cock Robin's love
To little Jenny Wren,
And when he got unto the end,
Then he began again."

Long ago, too, before the introduction of mechanical machinery on farms, people sang nursery rhymes to help with their daily chores. In order to persuade the cows to give more milk, the dairymaid sang:

"Cushy cow, bonny, let down thy milk,
And I will give thee a gown of silk;
A gown of silk and a silver tee,
If thou will let down thy milk to me."

And when she had enough milk, she put it in the butter churn, singing:

"Come, butter, come,
Peter's standing at the gate,
Waiting for a butter cake,
Come, butter, come."

illustrated by Belinda Lyon

The Donkey Brownie

by Anne Hughson

illustrated by Pamela Storey

On a sunny Saturday morning in September a battered animal truck rattled up the rough lane. Jennifer pushed open the gate to the field next to their cottage. Dad and the man in the truck let down the ramp and there stood the donkey.

The man took hold of the donkey's shaggy mane calling, "Come on there!" and carefully the donkey plodded down the ramp. Dad gave the sturdy creature a push towards the gateway, and the donkey obediently trotted through.

The three of them stood and watched as the donkey walked a few paces, then dropped his head to munch the green juicy grass.

Mum had seen an advert asking for winter homes for seaside donkeys. Mr Neville, the farmer for whom Dad worked, didn't mind his field being borrowed for a donkey while his cattle were inside for the winter.

"He's the last one to be delivered," the donkey man said. "I'm off home. I'll be back to collect him at Easter."

"What's his name?" Jennifer asked as the donkey man swung himself back into the truck.

"Brownie," the man shouted as he started the engine and drove away.

Brownie looked up at the noise, kicked his heels and galloped round the field.

Dad and Jennifer laughed.

"That donkey's going to enjoy his holiday," Dad said.

Jennifer often went to stand at the donkey's gate during that weekend. Each time she took a tasty titbit for him. The first time he ignored her, but next time he came to the gate and took a carrot from her outstretched hand. After that he trotted to the gate each time she appeared.

Before school on Monday morning Jennifer took Brownie an apple, and the first thing she did when she came home was to run to his gate. Brownie trotted over and Jennifer rubbed his rough coat, and patted his dusty sides.

Jennifer couldn't wait to tell Brown Owl about her donkey. She had been a Brownie for a year now, and was in the Gnomes. She was very keen to gain badges, and had four already — now she had a plan for the fifth.

"Brown Owl, could I take my Animal Lover's badge if I look after Brownie the donkey?" Jennifer asked.

Brown Owl thought this was an excellent idea. "You must keep a notebook of everything you do for him."

At the end of Brownies when they were all standing in a circle, little Jill, who had only just joined, said, "I wish we could all see Jennifer's donkey."

"Oh, yes!" the others chorused.

Diane, the Gnomes Sixer, said, "Couldn't the donkey be a sort of Pack mascot?"

"With a name like Brownie, he certainly should be," laughed Brown Owl.

Outside the village hall Jennifer skipped round with her friends calling last goodnights and goodbyes while Brown Owl talked to her Mum, who had been waiting in the car. During the drive home Mum said, "It seems Brownie is going to be a very popular donkey."

Jennifer told her mother all about the Animal Lover's badge.

Brownie didn't need extra food while there was still plenty of grass. Dad said that in the winter weather they would give him some hay. He showed Jennifer how to brush Brownie's thick coat. It was hard work! There was a drinking trough in the field which always had fresh water. Jennifer had to keep it clear of ice in frosty weather. There was an open ended shed in a corner, where Brownie could shelter from the wind and rain. Jennifer kept it cleaned out and laid fresh straw on the floor.

Sometimes she climbed onto Brownie's back for a ride round the field. Dad had put a barrel for her to stand on while she swung her leg over Brownie's broad back. She held onto Brownie's thick mane tightly and he plodded round as she bumped up and down.

All this she wrote in her donkey diary.

At the next Brownie meeting Brown Owl announced that next Saturday, if it was fine, they would go on a Pack outing, for a picnic in Brownie's field.

"So that was what Mum and Brown Owl were talking about," thought Jennifer.

The Brownies jumped up and down shouting excitedly. Brown Owl held up her hand for silence so that she could tell them more details.

Jennifer could have cried when she opened the curtains on Saturday morning to find the rain pouring down. At breakfast Dad came in from his early morning jobs and switched on the weather forecast.

"Clearing later," the weather man said confidently. Then the telephone rang. It was Brown Owl.

"Yes, we'll hope for the best and go ahead," Mum was saying.

The weather man was right. By lunch time the sun was trying to get out from behind the clouds.

At two o'clock the Brownies arrived, splodging up the puddle-filled lane in their wellingtons.

Jennifer and her dad were at the field gate to meet them. Brownie trotted over to see what all the chatter was about. Everyone crowded round to stroke and pat his shaggy coat which was growing thick for winter, and was still rough despite Jennifer giving him an extra thorough grooming that morning.

Little Jill was nervous at first, but Brown Owl held her up to stroke his soft ears.

All the Brownies wanted a ride, so Dad lifted them up in turn and each girl had a ride up the field and back.

Little Jill was afraid so Jennifer got onto Brownie and Brown Owl put Jill in front of her and Jennifer held Jill's waist with one hand and Brownie's mane with the other.

By then the Brownies were all hungry for their picnic tea which they had brought. Brown Owl gazed at their muddy boots, and the soaking wet grass.

"Where can we sit?" she wondered.

"I put clean straw down in Brownie's shed this morning," Jennifer suggested.

So they all went and sat on Brownie's straw bed, and ate their tea and sang songs until it was time to trudge back down the lane to the village.

But before they left, Brown Owl gave Jennifer a Gnomes Emblem, and a Brownie Promise Badge.

"Perhaps your dad could fix these in Brownie's shed," she said, "because I think after today Brownie the donkey is a real Brownie."

Jennifer gained her Animal Lover's badge just before Christmas. They were in the middle of practising for the Christmas play. This was a Pack Venture so Jennifer was looking forward to gaining a Venture badge. She was acting Joseph, and Diane was Mary. Joseph had to come onto the stage leading Mary, who was very tired after their long journey, to the innkeeper's door.

The stage had several doors leading off it. The

innkeeper's door led into a little room where they all changed into their costumes. On the opposite side of the stage was a door that said 'Emergency Exit' above it, and it led straight outside to some steps down to the car park.

It was while they were rehearsing that Jennifer had her important idea. After that she forgot her words several times because she was thinking of her idea instead of the rehearsal.

Afterwards she ran up to Brown Owl. "Brown Owl, in the Bible it says that Mary rode on a donkey. Couldn't Brownie be in our play?"

At first Brown Owl laughed. "Whatever next, a donkey in the village hall!"

"No, just on the stage," said Jennifer, who had been thinking it all out. "I could bring Brownie through the emergency exit."

Brown Owl became thoughtful. "I wonder," she said.

Mum was at the back of the hall waiting to take Jennifer home. Brown Owl went over to talk to her. Mum laughed too.

At the final dress rehearsal they decided to try it.

Dad said, "Now don't be disappointed, Jennifer, if Brownie won't go up those steps."

Dad had borrowed a trailer from the farm to take Brownie to the village. The night was freezing cold and as Dad guided the donkey down the ramp, Brownie's breath was white as puffs of mist. Jennifer came to the stage door in her costume with Diane. They had to stand outside with Dad till they heard the end of the opening hymn. Both girls had coats round their shoulders and stood close to Brownie's warm sides.

The singing ceased. Jennifer opened the exit door and Dad slapped Brownie's hind quarters. "Get on, boy," he said.

Jennifer took hold of his mane and called, "Come on, Brownie, remember you're a real Brownie."

The donkey clopped up the steps and stood in the doorway. Dad lifted Diane up and Jennifer held on to her as she led Brownie slowly across the stage to the innkeeper's door. After offering to show them his stable the innkeeper led Mary and Joseph and the donkey back to the exit door where Dad was waiting to hold Brownie again.

Jennifer hugged the donkey's neck. "He did it, Dad."

The next night the hall was full of people, buzzing with chatter and laughter. The first hymn was sung. All the lights went off. The curtain opened, the stage lights went on, and Joseph led Mary on a donkey to the innkeeper's door.

Later when the scene was the stable, and baby Jesus lay in the hay, Brownie stood quietly behind Joseph. Occasionally the donkey dipped his head to Joseph's shoulder, who put a hand to his muzzle and the donkey stood content again. Jennifer was hoping that her emergency supply of carrot pieces would last the evening.

At the end of the play she led Brownie back to the exit, and Dad took him to the trailer while another hymn was sung, so Brownie didn't take a bow in the final tableau when everyone clapped, and the angels, shepherds and kings looked at each other with pleased grins.

At the next Brownie meeting all the Brownies received their Venture badges and Jennifer was given two, one for herself, and one for the donkey, Brownie.

MAKE A MOUSE BOOKMARK

by Wendy Atkinson

illustrated by Chris Sheridan

You will need a small piece of grey felt
glue e.g. Copydex
sequins
string
cotton
spring-type hair clip

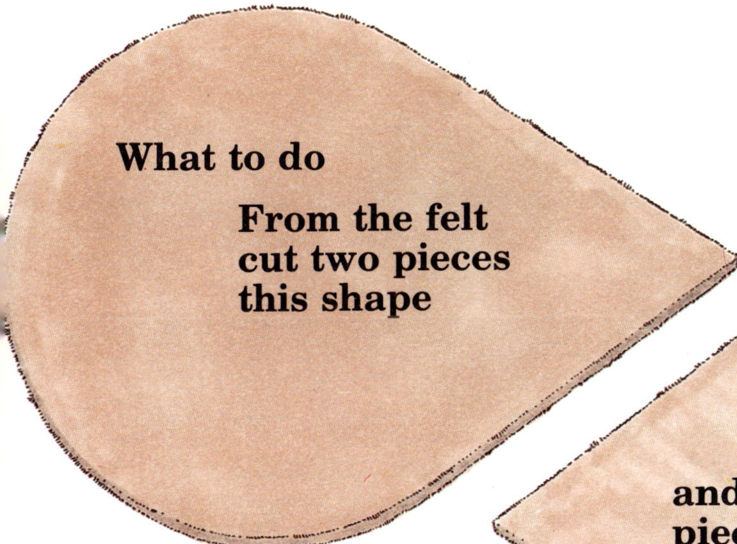

What to do

From the felt cut two pieces this shape

and one piece this shape

Fold the diamond shape in half and put the hair clip round it.

Glue round the edge of the body shape and place the diamond on top.

Place a length of string at the other end then place the other body piece on top.

Decorate with cotton whiskers sequin eye and felt ears and nose.

ROBINS FOR CHRISTMAS

the tradition behind this popular Christmas bird

by Peter Brown

The robin is a familiar sight around our gardens, with his orange-red breast and large dark eyes, and without doubt is the best known of all British birds.

His trusting manner and the way he comes to our doors in search of food in winter makes him well liked everywhere. It's not surprising that in 1961 the robin was officially chosen as the national bird of Britain.

However the robin is also a symbol of Christmas, as you can see if you look at a selection of Christmas cards. Almost 75% of all British Christmas cards have robins on them; no other creature appears on so many cards at any time of the year.

One reason for this is the prominent part played by robins in our Christmas traditions. According to legend the robin was originally a brown bird, who went to Bethlehem to see the birth of Christ. He helped to keep the baby warm by bringing feathers and small pieces of straw to the manger, and for this service was given a beautiful red breast. God said to the bird, "Blessed be thou, wherever thou goest happiness and joy shall follow thee; blue as the heaven shall be thy eggs, and from henceforth thou shalt be the bird of God."

During Queen Victoria's reign, when people first started sending Christmas cards, robins appeared on many of them. They were shown carrying letters in their beaks, knocking at doors, and lifting door knockers. Some cards showed robins flying with little letters hanging from their beaks, printed with the message, "A Happy Christmas", and "A Happy New Year".

Robins were shown carrying cards and letters on these early cards because postmen at the time wore red uniforms and were often nicknamed 'robins', even after their uniform changed to dark blue.

In addition, robins were used on Christmas cards because the vivid scarlet of the robin's breast was a cheerful colour for cards and looked striking against the white of the snow which invariably appeared on Victorian Christmas cards.

Later on during Queen Victoria's reign, robins were depicted on Christmas cards doing many other things besides carrying messages. They were seen skating on ice, pulling crackers, sitting on logs, and perching on Christmas cakes, as well as hopping about outside churches and being fed by small children in the snow.

They even appeared in uniforms on some cards. One showed a robin dressed as a soldier, and by pulling a tab attached to the card the robin-soldier could be made to march in a most life-like manner.

Another unusual card showed a bare snow scene, but when the card was held up to the light, a robin could be seen flying through the air. Special instructions inside the card told the reader how to find the robin:
"Behind the robin, but let the light fall,
In swarms his companions will come to his call".

Today we have forgotten why the robin was first chosen to appear on our Christmas cards, but he has never lost his popularity and still appears on many messages of goodwill to friends and relatives over the Christmas season.

CONSERVATION

by Alan Major

One of the clauses needed to gain this badge states that Brownies should collect seeds of native trees, which means those that have been growing in Britain's countryside for thousands of years, not those which come from other countries and are grown as ornamental trees in parks and gardens.

It also says the seeds of two species must be germinated and grown until the first true leaves appear. In Autumn, many trees bear and drop ripe seeds, sometimes in the form of berries and nuts, which are types of seeds. These can be collected. It is best to have each type of seed in its own bag, all the ash in one bag, the elm in another and so on, so that they are separate.

If you are not going to plant them within a few days of collecting them, place in paper bags (they keep better in these), and put in a dry cupboard or a large tin. If kept in plastic bags they may go mouldy. If any of the seeds feel damp after lying on the ground, place on a tray or tin lid in the sunshine, to dry out before storing. Most can be kept in bags until the following Spring, but others, such as oak acorns, sweet chestnuts and conkers of horse chestnut, which have a lot of food stored in them, begin to germinate soon after they fall on earth, and so must be planted quickly after collecting. When gathering these, it is also a good idea to collect some of the earth in a bag, to plant them in later. (Most of these seeds will grow in ordinary garden soil, except where there is a lot of chalk or clay, then other soil must be mixed in.)

1. Put some broken crockery and small stones in the bottom of each flower pot. Then almost fill with collected soil, or seed compost, which your parents may have in their greenhouse. Lightly water and allow this to soak through to settle the soil.
2. In a small pot put one seed on top of the soil. In a larger pot put two seeds, spaced apart. Try to place the seeds how they were when found on the earth. Acorns must be planted lying on their side; chestnuts and conkers with the flat base on the soil or compost. Cover with another layer of soil, press down and water again. Acorns and conkers should only be put one to a pot, as they need a lot of room to grow. As the clause states two different germinated species, plant several different kinds in their own pots in case some germinate quicker than others, or not at all. Put a label on the side of the pot, or a plastic tag pushed in the soil with the name of the seed on it.
3. Put the pots outside or in an unheated greenhouse, garage, or shed, keeping the soil damp, but not sticky wet. Or you can put a plastic bag over each pot with an elastic band to keep it in place, so the soil stays moist and does not need watering. Put in a shady, rather than a sunny place.
4. As soon as you see the tiny seedlings appearing with their seed leaves, remove the plastic bag. Still keep the soil damp (but not wet, otherwise the seedlings will rot and die). Watering once a week is usually enough now. The seed leaves are followed by the first pair of true leaves which will be like the other leaves on the tree.
5. If the pots are in a shed or greenhouse when the true leaves open wide, put them out in the garden if it is summer, but not if it is winter, when they should be kept indoors until Spring.
6. Your tester will ask about your plans for the tree seedlings. They can be planted in a garden if there is enough room for a tree to grow. If not, it is better to plant them in a wild place where they can grow big and healthy, adding to the number of trees in the area. In this way you will have done your important part in increasing and conserving trees in the countryside.

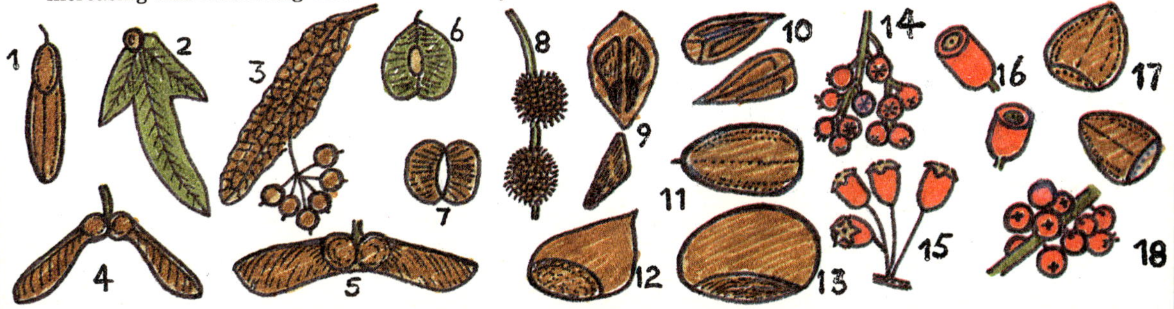

1. Ash. 2. Hornbeam. 3. Lime. 4. Sycamore. 5. Maple. 6. Elm. 7. Silver Birch. 8. Plane. 9. Scots Pine seeds, in pairs in a cone, and singly. 10. Beech. 11. Oak acorn. 12. Sweet Chestnut. 13. Horse Chestnut conker. 14. Rowan (Mountain Ash). 15. Hawthorn haws. 16. Yew. 17. Hazel nuts. 18. Holly.

The Story of Piggy Banks and Money Boxes

by Alan Major

This is a nineteenth century 'mechanical' bank. Put a coin in Santa's hand, and he will put it down the chimney.

Put a coin into the hand of this 'Dinah' bank, and she will throw it into her mouth.

Boxes in which to save money have been used for thousands of years. Roman children had pottery money boxes in which they kept coins. Although called 'boxes', they were made in many different shapes, including birds, animals, sheep, horses, cows, dogs, cats, hens, even fish. A popular money box was the shape of a standing or sitting down pig.

Five hundred years ago a pigg or pig was the name used for a pot, jar or crock used to hold things, and a piggery had nothing to do with real live pigs but was the pottery shop where the piggs could be bought from the pigwife, the woman who served in the shop. When pottery money boxes were made in animal shapes the name pigg for a jar or pot gave the potters the idea to model the box on a real pig.

As children often referred to a small pig as a piggy or piggie, and the money boxes in the shape of a pig were also little, they were known at first as piggies and later piggy boxes. In the Victorian era, saving was encouraged so that eventually the child would have enough money to put in the bank, so the pigs became known as piggy banks. The model pig had a slit in its back through which the coins were pushed.

The problem with the pottery money boxes was that, having put the coins in, it was difficult to get them out again. Often the only way to retrieve the money was to smash the piggy bank. Perhaps there were times when the piggy bank owner wanted a coin to buy sweets and when their mum or dad said *no*, the piggy bank was 'accidentally' dropped!

When Elizabeth the First was queen of England in the 16th century, money box pigs were made in red or brown clay. Later piggy banks were often made in the colours of the pigs reared on local farms and could be recognised by children. Many were all white or all black pigs, though there were black or brown spotted pigs as well. Colourful piggy banks were made too, blue, green, pink pigs, some with different coloured spots and stripes, made pretty so they were liked by children.

Apart from standing on four feet or sitting down, the piggy banks can have other differences. One of the potteries in Surrey in the 1890s was known for making piggy banks that were finely modelled and lifelike. This was because the potter was also a farmer and he modelled his pottery pigs on those in his farmyard. Sometimes the ears had a twist as if they were listening, or the lower lip of the mouth was curled so it looked as if the pig was smiling. Others, instead of having a slit for coins in its back, had a wide mouth for the coin to be put in, and so the coin was put in that. The first piggy banks only had a small slit as coins were then also small, but as coins were made larger so the slit was made longer, sometimes up to two inches long.

There were also curious fish-pig money boxes that had a very long body like a fish with scales, but with a pig's head and trotters, or a pig's body and trotters but with a fish's head and scales.

Pedlars used to sell piggy banks with other cheap pottery items from door to door in towns and cities, or they sold them on stalls at markets and fairs.

About a hundred years ago the first iron piggy banks were made, which meant that if accidentally or deliberately dropped, they did not break. Since then, piggy banks have been made in both metal and pottery. Some of the modern examples are large and gaily decorated, and are so attractive they are bought and used as ornaments not just as a means to save money.

Money boxes were made in other shapes, too. Those in the shape of country cottages were very popular, and sometimes churches and cathedrals were produced. The slit for the insertion of coins was in the roof. These were made for adults and were decorative, so they could be put on the mantel shelf or on a sideboard as an ornament. But small examples were also made in exactly the same shape for children, so that they could own a money box like Mum and Dad.

Other country objects were also made of pottery to use as money boxes. Household furniture in miniature was one sort, such as small wardrobes and chests of drawers. Others were milk churns, dovecotes, milestones and barrels. Figures of well-known local people were also used: the postman, the milkman, vicar, baker and so on, each carrying some item of their trade; the vicar a Bible, the postman letters, the baker bread. The slit for the coins was usually in the top of the head.

In the 1870s mechanical banks were introduced and became popular. These performed a feat when a coin was placed on, or in them. One of these was a figure of a football player who, when a coin was put on his foot, kicked it into a slit in the money box. Another was of a man who rolled his eyes after a coin was put in his mouth. A pony, when a coin was put in its mouth, tossed it into a manger. In another example a dog threw a coin through a hoop into a barrel. After a coin was put in the roof of a model bank a figure popped up from behind it to show a sign reading 'thank you'. There was even one, the Watchdog Safe, shaped like a safe on which sat a dog. A mechanism inside made the dog seem to bark when a coin was put in the safe's slit. There were money boxes made like Post Office pillar boxes. When the box was full a door in front opened or the lid was released and the money could be taken out.

From the start of this century until the 1930s, makers of sweets, toffee, chocolate and biscuits often put them in tins which, when all these things had been eaten, could be used as money boxes. Some of them were made in the shape of sweetshops with the name of the maker and advertisements for his sweets printed on the outside. There were also tins shaped like garages, railway stations, bus stations, farmyards, even buses and railway engines, which after being emptied could be used as a money box or a toy to play with.

There were also mechanical vending banks, which were slightly different. Wrapped sweets, toffees or bars of chocolate were contained in a metal box with a celluloid window behind which the tempting sweets and chocolate could be seen. When a coin was put in a sweet or bar of chocolate was supplied, rather like the vending machines in bus and railway stations and other public places today. By having to 'spend' a coin it meant the buyer saved the money and got a sweet or chocolate as a reward. Chocolate and sweet makers also put them in tins that looked like cash boxes, almost square with a handle. When a coin was put in a slit in the lid a mechanism released it so a sweet or chocolate could be taken out. Tins of tea were also made like money boxes.

Money boxes made like Post Office pillar boxes used for posting letters have been made for the past seventy years and are still being made. New ones have the initials of our Queen, ER II on them, but older ones can be dated by the initials of the king on the throne when they were made, either ER VII (Edward VII), GR V (George V) or GR VI (George VI).

Modern money boxes and piggy banks are worth keeping, undamaged if possible, as designs are changed and new ones introduced. If your Mum or Dad kept the money box they had as a child by now it could perhaps be worth a lot more money than any coins still inside it. There are people who collect them, attending auctions and antique sales to buy them just because they like their shapes or the way they work. Several toy museums in Britain have displays of money boxes so you can see how children saved their money in the past.

When a coin is fed into the bank, the skipping rope turns, and the girl's legs go up and down as she jumps over it.

Pictures by kind permission of Sotheby's, London.

Very, very

No-cook brownies

110g. plain chocolate
55g. butter
3 level tablespoons golden syrup
110g. sultanas or raisins
55g. chopped hazelnuts
55g. chopped glacé cherries

Melt chocolate in a basin over hot water, add butter, stir till melted. Mix in remaining ingredients. Put in tin, leave until set, then cut into squares.

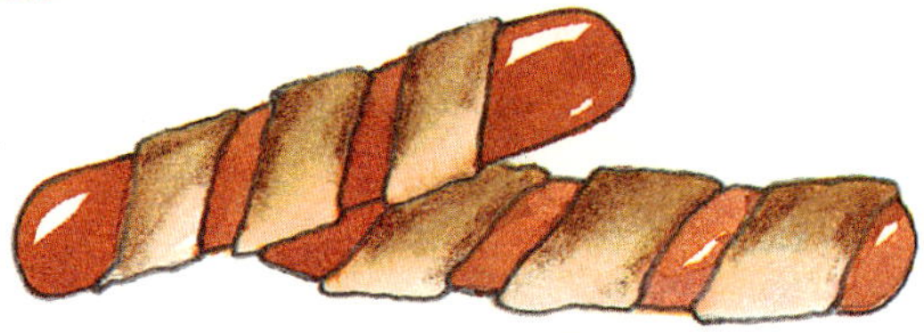

Sausage twists

225g. shortcrust pastry
8 large sausages
1 egg

Roll out pastry and cut into strips 30cm. x 10cm. Twist each strip round a sausage and brush with beaten egg. Bake on a greased baking sheet for 20 mins. at 220°C (425°F, gas mark 7).

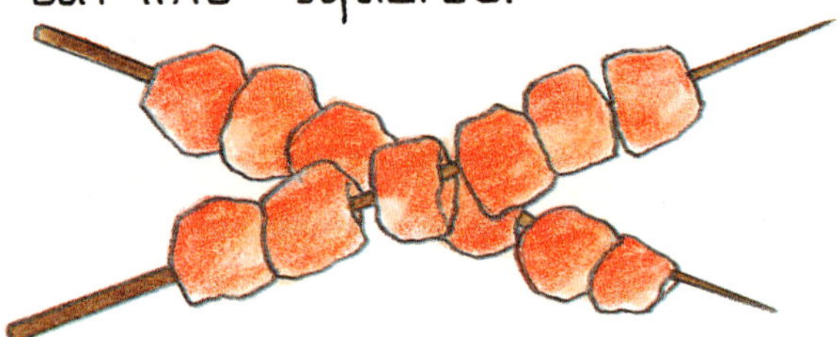

Chicken kebabs

2 boned chicken breasts, skinned and cut into chunks
1 carton plain yoghurt
juice of 1 lemon
1cm. cube of fresh ginger (or ½ tsp. ground)
1 clove garlic
salt, pepper, red food colouring

Roll the chicken pieces in lemon juice and leave for 30 mins. Grate the ginger and garlic and mix both with the yoghurt, salt and pepper and a few drops of food colouring. Pour over the chicken pieces and leave for 4 hours (or overnight). Thread the chicken pieces onto skewers and grill for about 10 mins, until cooked through and slightly crisp.

Marmite Wheels

225g. shortcrust pastry
marmite

Roll out pastry and spread with marmite. Roll up and cut into 1cm. slices. Bake at 220°C (425°F, gas mark 7) for 10 mins.

easy cooking!

by Jil Shipley

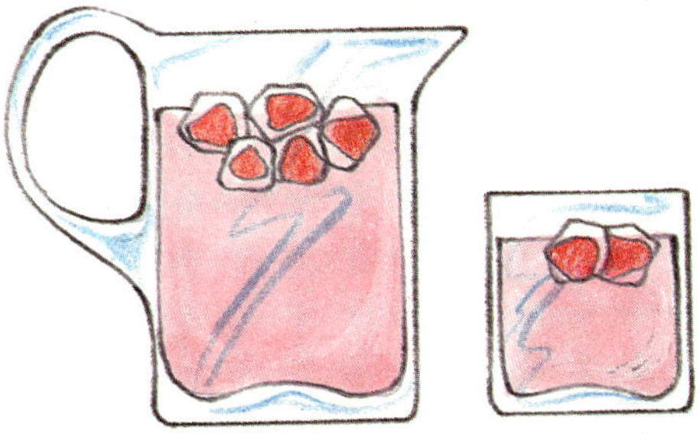

Strawberry lemonade

1 bottle lemonade
1 can strawberries

Drain the strawberries. Put one strawberry into each section of an ice-making tray. Fill with water and freeze. Mix the remaining strawberry juice with the lemonade in a jug and add the ice-cubes.

Cinnamon Roll-ups

110g. cream cheese
55g. caster sugar
9 slices brown or white bread
85g. butter
1 teaspoon cinnamon

Mix the cheese with 30g. sugar. Trim the crusts off the bread and roll each slice with a rolling pin until very thin. Spread the cheese and sugar mix onto the bread and roll up. Cut each roll in half. Melt the butter and mix together the remaining sugar and cinnamon. Brush each roll with butter and roll in sugar/cinnamon mixture until well coated.
Bake on a rack at 230°C (450°F, gas mark 8) for 30 mins. until very crisp.

Cinder toffee

110g. sugar
2 tablespoons golden syrup
30g. butter
1 teaspoon bicarbonate of soda

Melt butter, sugar and syrup in a large saucepan and boil without stirring for 5 mins, until the mixture begins to turn brown. BE VERY CAREFUL. BOILING SUGAR CAN BURN. Remove from heat and mix in the bicarbonate of soda, stirring well. Pour into a well greased tin and leave to set. When cool, cut into squares.

Kung Hei Fat Choy!

恭祝
新年快樂

by Susan Winter

In Britain the new year always starts on 1st January, but for Chinese people the new year can fall any time between mid-January and mid-February. This is because the Chinese calendar is based on the moon's cycle. Each year is named after one of twelve animals: the rat, ox, tiger, rabbit, dragon, snake, horse, sheep, monkey, cockerel, dog and pig. 1986 is the year of the tiger.

In China, Singapore, Hong Kong and every place where Chinese people live, children are told this legend of how the years were given their names.

One day twelve animals were arguing. They wanted the new year to have a name.

"It should be named after me," crowed the cockerel. "I wake everyone at the beginning of the day."

"It should be called the Year of the Monkey," screeched monkey. "I am the cleverest of the animals."

"Nonsense," roared the dragon. "I have magic powers, it must be named the Year of the Dragon."

And so the argument went on, with the animals getting more and more noisy.

Now the gods had been listening to the argument and they became so annoyed with the animals that at last one of them boomed, "Be quiet!" in a voice that echoed around the jungle. Tiger stopped roaring, pig stopped squeaking, dog stopped barking. They all stopped arguing and listened.

"Why don't you go to the great river and race across?" suggested the god. "This year will be named after the winner of the race."

The animals agreed that this was a good idea and rushed to the river bank. With much pushing and squabbling they lined up. "Ready, steady, go!" cried the gods. SPLASH! In jumped the twelve, and started to swim as fast as they could to the other side.

Ox was very strong and he was soon out in front of all the others. But rat, although small, was very clever. When the animals had jumped into the river he had caught hold of ox's tail and had been towed across. Now he pulled himself on to ox's back, crept up to ox's shoulder and waited. Just as ox reached the bank rat leapt on to the grass.

"I've won, I've won," he squeaked.

"How did you do that?" ox asked in astonishment.

Rat laughingly explained, and ox laughed too. The gods announced, "Rat is the winner, so this will be the Year of the Rat. Next year will be called the Year of the Ox."

All the other animals finished the race and around the edge of this page you will see the order they came in.

Chinese people believe that your personality takes on some of the characteristics of the animal your birth year is named after. Look at the chart opposite and see if you agree.

February 1972– 2nd February 1973	Rat	Rat people are charming, ambitious, thrifty and persistent.	8th February 1978– 27th January 1979	Horse	Popular and cheerful people who enjoy parties.
3rd February 1973– 23rd January 1974	Ox	People born in this year are easy going, quiet and clever with their hands.	28th January 1979– 15th February 1980	Sheep	People born in a sheep year are shy but like to help others and are creative.
24th January 1974– 10th February 1975	Tiger	If you are born in tiger year you are courageous but can be selfish.	16th February 1980– 4th February 1981	Monkey	Chatterboxes, but successful and full of common sense.
11th February 1975– 30th January 1976	Rabbit	These people are clever in business and in handling money. They can be tearful.	5th February 1981– 24th January 1982	Cockerel	Hard workers who like to succeed. They can be reckless.
31st January 1976– 17th February 1977	Dragon	Dragons are healthy, energetic, courageous, sensitive and honest.	6th February 1970– 26th January 1971	Dog	Loyal and hard working, they can keep a secret but can be obstinate.
18th February 1977– 7th February 1978	Snake	Very wise, deep thinkers; they don't like to fail.	27th January 1971– 18th February 1972	Pig	Brave, polite and kind people; they make good friends.

1 Brightly coloured masks lie waiting

2 The dancers put on their costumes

10 . . . and wishes you all a happy New Year

Preparations for Chinese New Year start weeks in advance, when children help their parents to clean every corner of their home. Rugs are brushed, windows cleaned and paintwork washed, to make certain the house or flat is clean enough for the spirits of the new year to enter. Then all the rooms are decorated with red paper decorations and lanterns. Red is thought to be an especially lucky colour.

At midnight fire crackers are let off in the streets to frighten away the spirits of the old year. The next few days are a holiday for everyone, with schools, shops and offices closed. Families prepare and eat large meals with many special foods being shared. One speciality is dumplings made from rice flour and almonds; they are delicious when eaten hot. Parents give their children scarlet envelopes decorated with good luck messages and pictures of lions and dragons painted in gold. Inside there is money for the children to save, or to spend on clothes and toys.

9 The lion bows and flutters his eye-lids at the end of his dance

8 A Chinese lion-dance band

3 . . . and the lion moves off

The New Year celebrations shown here were organised by Poons Restaurant, Covent Garden, London, to raise money for children's charities. The Brownie Annual would like to thank Mr and Mrs Poon and Rachel Macdonald for their help in planning this feature.

4 The lion roars at the watching people

If you are lucky enough to live in or near London, Leicester or cities where many people with a Chinese background have settled, you might see and hear some new year street celebrations. Led by a band of beating drums and crashing cymbals, a "lion" dances its way through the streets. This is no ordinary lion but highly trained dancers moving underneath a huge, brightly coloured mask and long train of richly embroidered and sparkling cloth. They make the lion dip, sway and rise to the music.

The lion pauses outside shops where the owners have strung a line on which is pegged new money and a cabbage! He bows, then raises his head and opens his jaws. With one loud snap the money and cabbage are gone, the money to pay the dancers, the cabbage to feed the hungry lion. The shop owners are overjoyod by eating the food and taking their money, the lion has brought them good luck and prosperity for the new year.

5 To reach the lucky money and cabbage, the dancers stand on each others' shoulders

7 Two lions dance above the crowd

6 New Year banners

The Swimming Pool Adventure

by Margaret Baird

illustrated by Gay Galsworthy

Helen woke up suddenly, and remembered she was going with the Brownies to the seaside for the day. On her chair were her yellow t-shirt and brown shorts, which she had ironed carefully the night before.

"Helen!" her mother called. "Time to get up!"

Helen jumped out of bed and put on her clothes. She chose a pair of clean white socks, and laced up her plimsolls.

Downstairs, breakfast was ready, and her father was eating scrambled eggs on toast. Helen sat down at the table, and read through the *The Brownie* magazine which had come inside the morning paper.

"Your packed lunch is in the kitchen," Mrs Collins said as she put down a plateful of egg and toast in front of Helen.

Helen reached for the salt, and sprinkled it onto her eggs. "Is it ham sandwiches for lunch?" she asked. "Can I have a chocolate biscuit as well, please? Brown Owl said to take plenty of food, because we won't be home until six o'clock."

"It's all ready," said her mother. "I've been up since seven-thirty, packing it up for you." She sighed and poured a cup of tea for Mr Collins.

"Are you feeling all right?" he asked. "It seems to me you're doing too much for Helen. She could pack up her own lunch, couldn't she?"

Helen felt cross. She pushed away her breakfast. "I'll have to go," she said. "I'm calling at Mary's house at a quarter to nine."

She put on her anorak, and changed into her leather sandals. Her lunch box was in the kitchen, and she collected her bag with her swimming things ready packed into it. Her mother waved goodbye from the window as Helen walked down the front path. Helen felt guilty. Her mother's face looked pale and tired. Then she forgot her worries as she ran along the pavement, and turned into Blake Terrrace, where her friend Mary lived.

It was just after a quarter to nine now, so she should be ready and waiting. Helen knocked on the blue front door, which opened straight onto the street. Mary opened the door, carrying her little brother, Jake, in her arms. She didn't have her Brownie uniform on.

"Aren't you ready?" asked Helen in surprise.

Mary looked upset, and put Jake down on the floor. Jake was three. He was blue-eyed, and very noisy. "I can't come. Mum's had to go to work, and I've got to look after Jake. Mrs Martin from next door promised to keep an eye on us." She picked up her little brother again, to stop him running out onto the road. Helen felt upset. They had been looking forward to the trip to the seaside for weeks. Mary's family didn't go away for

holidays, so she hardly ever had a day out.

"Let's ask Brown Owl if Jake can come too!" Helen said.

Mary shook her head. "Mum would say no," she said. "Jake's too little for such a long day. You go, Helen. I'll see you tomorrow."

Helen thought about being a Brownie, and remembered the Brownie Law. Suddenly she decided what to do. She told Mary to wait at home, while she ran to the church hall to tell Brown Owl that neither she nor Mary could go. They were *both* going to look after Jake for the day.

At the church hall, Brown Owl was in the coach, checking her list to see who was missing. Helen explained what had happened.

"What a kind Brownie you are," said Brown Owl.

The coach roared off, and Helen waved to all her friends. She felt sad, but started walking back to Mary's house, calling at home first, to tell her mother.

Back at Mary's terraced house, it was warm and sunny in the kitchen. Jake threw his bricks at Helen while Mary poured out glasses of milk for them. "'Scuse the mess," she said. "Mum left in a rush."

She put on an apron, and together they washed up the dishes, and brushed the floor.

"Beds next," said Mary. "Then a walk with Jake before lunch."

Helen's eyes shone. "This is fun," she said. "It's like having a sister!"

They made the beds, and dusted the furniture. Then Helen cleaned the bath, and Mary brushed the stairs. Jake ran about, helping to dust with the bright yellow duster that Mary had given him. Soon the house was shining and tidy.

"He'll be a good Cub!" said Helen. They laughed, and then Mary picked Jake up, and strapped him into his blue and white striped pushchair. Mary popped next door to tell Mrs Martin where they were going, and she waved them off.

"Orange?" he said hopefully. They decided to take him to the cafe in the park, where they could buy him a drink. Helen helped push him along the footpath, and soon they reached the playground. They all had a drink of orange, and then Jake shouted to go on the swings. He went on the chute, and played on the climbing frame.

"He must be tired by now," said Helen, who was feeling ready for her lunch.

Mary caught Jake as he swung, monkey-like, on the climbing frame. He screamed as he was put into his pushchair, but Mary firmly pushed him home. "He's hungry," she said.

Helen planned lunch for the three of them as they walked back. She had plenty of ham sandwiches to share, and Jake would enjoy the chocolate biscuit. They had a picnic, sitting out in the little garden at the back of the house.

"I was going to have fish and chips," Mary said.

"This is much more fun."

Jake banged his spoon on his plate and sang. Helen laughed. "He likes ham sandwiches too," she said, but that reminded her about the argument at home, and she felt unhappy.

Then Jake upset his orange juice all over himself, so she soon forgot about the argument again. They changed Jake into blue and white striped dungarees and a clean t-shirt.

"Let's take him swimming," Helen suggested. Her family belonged to the sports club, so she could take them there free. They checked with Mrs Martin that it was all right, packed their

towels and costumes into Helen's rucksack, and set off. On the way they stopped at Helen's house to collect her membership card and tell her mum where they were going.

Soon they reached the sports club, and Helen showed her card. Mary took Jake into her cubicle, and put on his costume, while Helen changed.

The club's baths were very modern, and every half hour a machine sent a huge wave of water up the large pool. The three of them splashed in the shallow pool and threw a beach ball to one another. Helen was a strong swimmer, so she set off to swim in the big pool.

"Watch me dive into the diving pool," she said to Mary. She posed on the board, and dived in. Then she went back down to the shallow pool.

Mary rushed up to her. "I've lost Jake!" she shouted. "I was watching you dive, and he must have run off!"

Nearly in tears, she ran back into the changing rooms to look for him. Helen felt cold and sick inside. She went up to the attendant on the bathside, and he rang the alarm. All the swimmers stopped as the message boomed over the loudspeaker.

"Emergency — a small boy in blue bathing trunks is lost. Please search everywhere, and bring him to reception."

It was like a bad dream. Helen felt it was all her fault. If only she hadn't shown off her diving! She shivered, and the attendant told her to change and have a hot drink.

Miserably, Helen walked back into the changing room, looking everywhere for little Jake. Then she had an idea — perhaps he had gone to find some orange juice. At the public baths, where Mary usually took him, the cafe was upstairs. She saw some steps leading up to a door, which said: STAFF ONLY. Helen pushed open the door and walked along the passage. The message came over the loudspeaker again. "Emergency! Emergency!"

Then she heard a chuckling noise — just like Jake's laugh. It came from inside a small storeroom. There was Jake, trying to reach a shelf which was stacked with bottles of squash and cartons of crisps.

"Orange?" he said. Helen picked him up, and walked as quickly as she could down to the attendant's office. Jake tried to wriggle out of her arms as he saw Mary in the office. Everyone was very glad Jake had been found, and the attendant announced to all the swimmers he was safe.

Helen changed into her shorts and t-shirt, and Mary put Jake back into his dungarees. Then they went into the cafe, and Helen bought a bar of chocolate and milk for them all.

Mary soon looked better. "We'd better go home, now," she said. "Mum will be back from work soon. Wait till I tell her about my exciting day!"

They pushed Jake back home, and he fell asleep in his pushchair. Mary lifted him up and carried him to his cot. Helen had an idea. "Let's make tea, ready for your mum," she said.

So they put the kettle on, and made sandwiches, and set the table. Helen put on her anorak, and said goodbye.

"Thank you for staying with me," said Mary. "One day, can I come and help you at your house?" Then Jake woke up and cried, so she waved goodbye and shut the door.

Helen let herself in the front door of her house. It seemed very quiet and tidy everywhere. She missed Jake.

"Hello, Mum! It's me!" she shouted.

Her mother had her feet up in the lounge. She got up. "I'll start cooking tea," she said. "You must be tired after helping Mary all day."

Helen put on an apron, and went into the kitchen. "I'll cook tea," she shouted. "I'm going to help at home much more now."

At Brownies that week, Mary and Helen told Brown Owl all about their day out.

"How about taking your Cook and House Orderly badges?" she suggested. "I can see you've had plenty of practice."

Helen's mother came in to see Brown Owl at the end of the meeting, and Helen told her about the badges she was going to take. Mrs Collins smiled at Brown Owl. "That's good," she said. "I'm going to need an extra pair of helping hands around the house, when Helen's new baby sister or brother arrives!"

THEATRE

Did you realise that nearly all theatres throughout the country have cats? These cats are called 'working cats' or 'house cats' by the actors, since they earn their keep by being excellent mousers and so the theatres are completely free of rats and mice.

At one time, 'working cats' were seen in every city and town, in warehouses, shops, and offices, where they made sure that mice were never a problem.

But today, cats are usually seen only in theatres, where by long tradition the payroll includes a weekly allowance to buy the best food for them. This often means the choicest bits of fish and tenderest of meat.

Some actors and actresses are very superstitious, and believe that a cat of any colour brings good luck to a play on the stage. If a play is not successful, many actors will blame the theatre for not keeping a cat.

The sleek and well-fed theatre cats are almost natural actors themselves: they are usually most elegant in appearance and conscious of their good looks, and not timid at all — very much like actors and actresses!

However, these lovable cats can be naughty sometimes, and will decide to take part themselves on the stage. One cat once decided to walk on the set without any warning, inspected all the furniture on the stage, jumped down into the orchestra pit, and then slinked its way into the stalls where it sat down to watch the rest of the play.

The audience were so amused by its antics that they gave it a round of applause, and the actors later complained that it had really stolen the show from them!

Not all theatre cats are showy and bold, though. Some are more shy, and the only time the audience sees them is when they take it upon themselves to bolt across the stage during a show. Such odd appearances can make the actors quite nervous — and it's even been

We found Dumpling in the props and scenery store, below the stage at the Ambassadors Theatre, where she lives.

She liked being stroked, and didn't mind when the Brownies (from the 10th City of London and 4th Clerkenwell Packs) sat on her cardboard box.

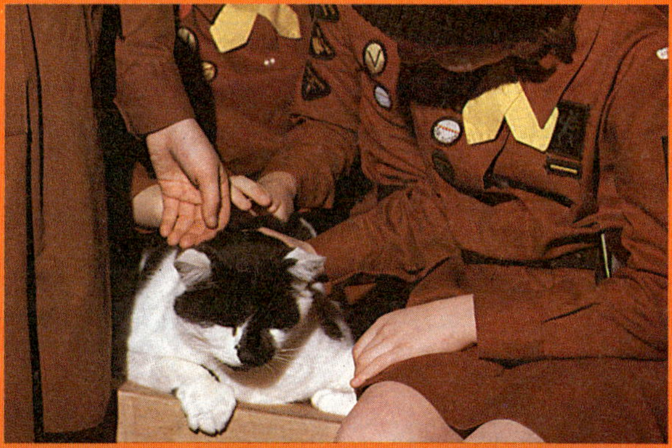

Ambrose, the Theatre Royal, Drury Lane cat, seemed to enjoy watching rehearsals.

Our thanks to Nigel Everret and James Gerson of the Strand Theatre, David Blyth of the Theatre Royal, Drury Lane, and Charles Stephens of the Ambassadors Theatre, for all their help with this feature.

CATS

by David Watkins

known for some to forget their lines as they are disturbed by the appearance of a cat on the stage.

Some theatre cats keep well out of sight during a performance, and only make their appearance when the crowds have gone home. The more mischievious cats, which insist on showing off in front of an audience, have to be locked up in the dressing rooms until the show is over.

When a show closes down and the theatre remains empty for a short while, it's the custom to take the cat to another theatre so that it is not lonely whilst waiting for the next show to open. Bouncer — one of London theatreland's most well-known cats — has travelled in this way to most of the theatres in the city, and always has a warm welcome since he is such an affectionate and loving cat.

How much does a cat cost a theatre per week to keep in food? Most theatres will allow about five pounds for food, but if a theatre is doing really well with packed audiences every night then this sum is increased to as much as six or seven pounds.

So it's no wonder that most theatre cats are fat and well looked after. After all, the friendly doorkeeper or stagehand keeps a good eye on them, and accepts it as a part of the job to shop for food for the cat during a break in the show.

When a theatre cat dies (usually at a good old age), the theatre staff will advertise through newspapers for a new cat. The advertisement might read something like this: "West End theatre has vacancy for backstage cat. Regular wages for food, good mousing opportunities — and some possibilities of taking part in the show".

Theatre cats lead very privileged and interesting lives, and seem to be proud of their title 'house cat' in some of the most famous theatres of the world.

photographs by Tony Rose

The view from a box is even better!

The Brownies agree!

He enjoyed showing off, and proudly walked across the stage for us.

There is a very grand bar at Drury Lane, and Ambrose made himself at home on one of the velvet seats.

Smoky came with us on a backstage tour of the Strand Theatre, where he lives. Like Dumpling, he can usually be found in the store-room beneath the stage, where there are lots of warm pipes to curl up on. He is shown with Mr Gerson, who looks after him.

BROWNIES' OWN

MUM

Mum is special in every way,
She makes the cakes every day,
Then we have our lunch, which is fishes,
Then She washes up our dishes.
But when it's her birthday she stays in
Bed, And pulls the blankets over her head,
Then she decides to wait and see,
If Someone will bring her a cup of tea.

This poem was written by Kirstine Sarah Tomlin of 25th Reading Pack.

Emma Webster of Poulshot in Wiltshire made up this story.

Carol Arnold of 4th Shirley Brownie Pack painted this clown.

Lighthouse painting by Lisa Cook of 1st Catforth Pack.

I am a seed and one day a farmer
came and bought me. I was a sun-
flower seed. The farmer was carrying me
in his pocket. The was all sorts of
rubbish in there. There was tissues,
old sweets, bits of string and other
things aswell. When we got to the
farmhouse the farmer planted me
in some soil in a flower pot. It
was very cold and dark in the soil
I could see no colours and I was
very sad. The farmer left me in
the flower pot for days and nights
The nights were even more dark
in the soil and one night I grew
a tiny root. Then a few other nights
I began to grow more roots and one
ay I grew a tiny shoot on top of me
nd I began to see some colours.
could see trees, flowers and bushes.
n one day the farmer came to
k a me and he said that I was
ving very well. Then the next night
w one leaf and I could hear
s. I could hear the birds singing
ars zooming by on the road-
could hear people whistling.
xt night I grew two more
o. now I had three leaves
e next night the farmer
look at me and I was
ful sunflower.

This poem was written by
Zöe East of 1st Spixworth
Brownie Pack.

A Rainy Day.

Pitter Patter goes the rain
Trickling down the
window. pane,
Dark clouds are drawing
near,
People outside begin to
fear.

Red, yellow, blue and
green
Coloured Umbrellas have
begun to be seen.
People outside are
coming in,
The thunder is making an
awful din.

Oh at last!
The sun is shining.
There is a rainbow in
the sky,
There are lots of pretty
colours,
Way up high.

by Kirstie Fieldhouse
of the 1st Sutton Coldfield Pack.

I have a little mouse
With eyes of pinky - white;
I can hold her in my hand
But I must not hold her tight.

PRESENTS TO MAKE

by Jil Shipley

Make candle-holders with self-hardening clay (Das). Make two balls of clay, damp them and press them together. Push a candle into the head, then add arms, nose, ears, damping each little piece of clay as you stick it on. Finish off the shape with a modelling tool or a knife. Pull out the candle, leave to dry, then paint and varnish.

Make some 'Antique' gold coins and turn them into jewellery. Design your coin then trace it onto a piece of card. Paint P.V.A. glue along the lines of the design and leave to dry. Then paint over the whole coin with gold paint – you'll need two coats. When the paint is dry cover the whole design with black poster paint, then press a piece of newspaper over the paint – this will lift off some paint and give the antique finish. When all the paint is dry cut out the coin and paint the back and edges with gold paint. Cut holes in the coins and thread them onto a piece of coloured cord, alternating the coins with pieces of macaroni painted gold or a contrasting bright colour.

Buy a small packet of bird seed. Roll little balls of peanut butter in the seed and push them into an open pine cone. Give it to a bird lover to hang from a branch for the blue-tits.

for yourself and your friends

Make a beautiful "Stained Glass" window decoration. Put a piece of white kitchen roll onto an old newspaper and dab on splodges of red, blue and yellow ink, totally covering the tissue. Hang it up to dry. Fold a square of black paper in four and cut out a simple design. Stick the cut-out shape onto the coloured tissue. Cut away the edges of the tissue and hang up the decoration, with cord, in a window where the light will shine through all the colours, just like stained glass!

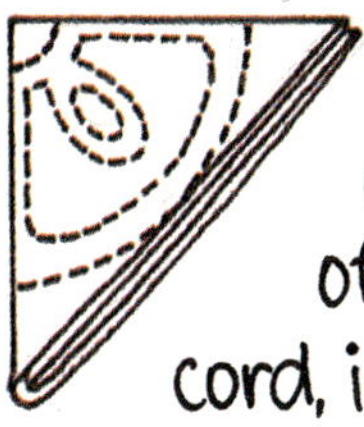

Well scrubbed smooth stones make lovely pets! Stick heads to bodies with a glue stick and draw on eyes with felt pens. You can varnish them if you like.

Make Grandma a book all about yourself. Use a long strip of paper, folded, or several small sheets sellotaped together. Cut a front and back cover a little bigger than the sheets inside. Glue the cover onto each end. Inside the book put lots of information about yourself – where you go to school, what you like to eat, photographs, your favourite colour. Decorate the cover with pretty wallpaper or paint or draw a design on it. Grandma will love it!

THINGS TO MAKE with WALNUTS

Ask a grown-up to help you to slit open some walnuts.
Eat the nuts. Now you have lots of half shells to make little gifts.

Make a doll in a cradle.

You need some scraps of fabric to make the doll and her bedding. Cut an 8cm. square of thin cotton and put a little ball of cotton wool in the centre. Tie a piece of cotton round the ball to form a head. Draw eyes, nose and mouth with a fine felt-tip pen and sew a couple of loops of thread onto the head for hair. Now tuck up the doll on a mattress of cotton wool with a pretty flowery sheet over her.

Fill the empty shells with little sweets and glue the shells together again with a glue stick.

Make a little boat for your brother. You need an empty shell, a used match and some coloured paper cut into sail shapes. Stick the sails to the match with a glue stick, then stick the match into the shell with plasticine or blu-tack. Make a whole fleet, they float beautifully.

FRUITY FELT JEWELLERY

Try making some felt fruit jewellery – all you need is: some squares of coloured felt thread, cotton wool or kapok for stuffing, and safety pins.

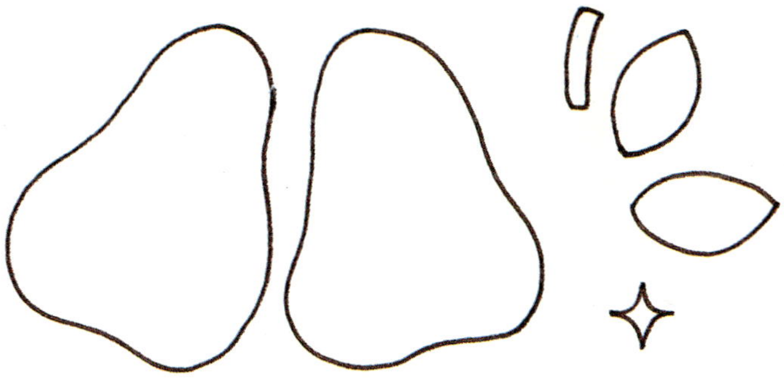

Draw your chosen fruit on paper first – try apples, pears, bananas, cherries – and cut out the outline to use as a pattern. Cut out the pieces in felt – two pieces of fruit, a stalk, one or two leaves and a star for the base.

Backstitch or overstitch the two fruit shapes together, leaving a little gap at the top, into which stuff some cottonwool or kapok – not too much, just enough to make a slightly plump shape. Over-sew the gap. Stitch on the stalk, then the leaves and the little star at the bottom. Then turn the fruit to its less attractive side and sew a safety pin onto this. Make two or three different fruits and wear them together.

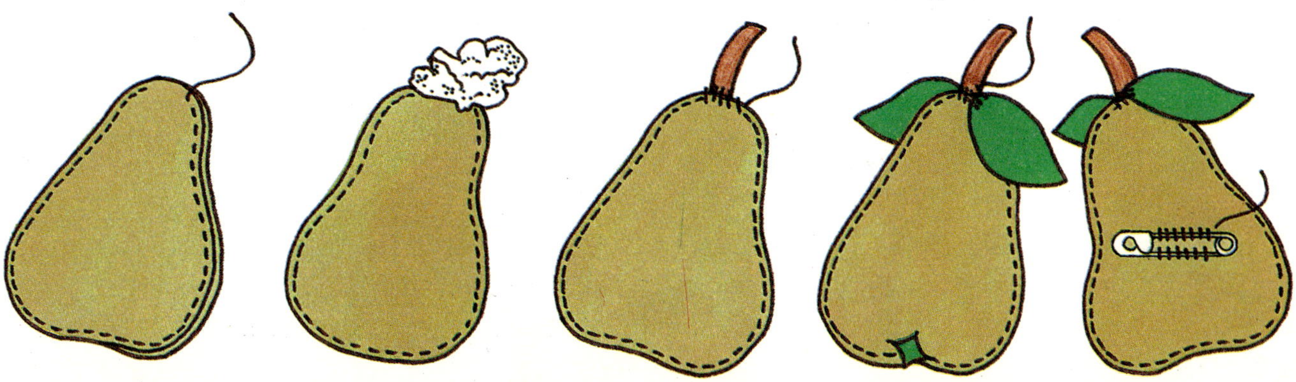

AMAZING MAZES

by Alan Major

The maze shown here is at Hatfield House, in Hertfordshire. It was planted in 1841.

I wonder if you ever have fun attempting the printed maze on the Puzzles Page of *The Brownie*? This has a starting entrance in one corner or at one side of it from which lead various lines or routes in different zig-zag directions, all leading to closed ends or lines – except the correct one, which goes eventually, after many twists and turns, to the object at the finish, usually in another corner or on the other side from the start. This is known as a picture maze and they have been enjoyed by children since children's magazines started in the 19th century.

You may be surprised to know, however, that Roman children over two thousand years ago played a similar game, called the Game of Troy, marking out the playing area of the maze with stones gathered in fields. The Maze was probably brought to Britain by the Romans when they invaded in 43AD and occupied our country for over three hundred years, being played by the sons and daughters of the Roman officers and soldiers.

But the idea of a maze is much older. The Ancient Egyptians built a maze which they called a Labyrinth that had three thousand rooms, half of them underground, the other half above ground. On the island of Crete in the Mediterranean is a Labyrinth which, according to Greek mythology, was built to confine Minotaur, the monster with the head of a bull and body of a man.

After the Romans left Britain in 406AD the maze puzzle game was forgotten, until reintroduced by the Normans in 1066. At Woodstock, Oxfordshire, Henry II created a bower and a maze during his reign in the 12th century.

Mazes were also known by other names such as Mizmaze, meaning a place of puzzlement and confusion, and Troy Towns, which came from the name of the Roman children's game.

The farmhouse garden at Troy Farm, Somerton, Oxfordshire, has an oval shaped maze, measuring 17m (57ft) by 15m (50ft) and surrounded by shrubs and trees. The maze is made of banks and ditches with 365m (400yds) of path inside to reach the centre, but it is an easy maze and impossible to get lost in.

At Breamore, Hampshire, is a medieval mizmaze cut in turf on Breamore Down that was used for religious rituals. At Troytown on St Agnes, an island in the Scilly Isles, there is a maze made with pebbles picked up locally. Some say it was made in 1729 by a bored lighthouse keeper to pass the time, but others think it is much older and dates back to the Bronze Age.

Down through the centuries mazes were made in various ways and for several purposes. Sometimes they were cut in turf, sited near a church. It is believed these were intended as a sort of punishment for sinners, who perhaps had not attended church services regularly or paid the taxes due to the church. The offender was blindfolded, put in the centre of the maze, and then had to find his way out again to the jeers and insults from the other villagers. To make sure the offender kept on the path of the maze and did not step over the banks to escape, the villagers had long poles which they used to prod the sinner back on to the path.

Other mazes made at this time were used as a sort of penance for those people in the village or small town who had failed to fulfil a vow, which many had to take, to be a pilgrim to the Holy Land. Crawling on hands and knees they had to find their way to the centre while reciting prayers and shouting their sin for all to hear. Another use was during May Day revels and other country festivities, in a game called Treading the Maze, which was held between several people, such as a swain and his girlfriend, who began on the outside and tried to be the first couple to reach the maze centre without crossing from one path to another or coming to a dead-end. William Shakespeare mentions mazes in *A Midsummer Night's Dream*, with Titania complaining to Oberon that, "The quaint mazes in the green for lack of tread are undistinguishable," meaning that the grass turf maze was so overgrown it could not be seen.

Many of the circular or square mazes which were originally deeply cut into the turf on a village green, meadow, common, or near a holy well, with banks higher than the paths on either side, were eventually destroyed for various reasons. The land may have been wanted for another use and Cromwell had many filled-in during the mid-17th century for religious reasons. Only the names Troy, Troy Town or Mizmaze may now survive as place or farm names to reveal that that was where there used to be a maze.

Fortunately not all the very old mazes were destroyed and in the 17th century it became fashionable for rich people who owned mansions to have a maze created on their country estates. These mazes were made with yew, box, juniper, privet, holly and other evergreen shrubs and trees to form timmed hedges, tall enough so they were above the height of the people trying to find their way in them, and to prevent people from looking over the top to see the way. Such mazes were a form of entertainment and amusement for visitors. A few of the mazes were also created with fruit-bearing shrubs and trees, "to a man's height, so as to make him wander in gathering berries and other fruits, such as apples and pears, until he cannot find his way out without help". Perhaps people didn't mind being lost in these mazes!

If you want to try a maze there are quite a lot in various parts of the country. One of the most famous is the Hampton Court Maze with 2 m (7 ft) high yew hedges, triangular in shape, with over 0.80 km (½ mile) of paths inside. It was planted about 1700 but who did it is not known. Over two hundred thousand people visit it every year. While the maze is open there is a park keeper on duty to go to the rescue of people who get lost and cannot find their way to the exit. At closing time he tours the maze to make sure it is empty!

At Alkborough, Humberside, there is a maze 13 m (44 ft) in diameter cut into turf near the church. Its origin is unknown but probably dates back to the 12th century, one suggestion being that it was cut by monks of Spalding Priory. It is called Julian's Bower, this name probably coming from Iulus, one of the characters who plays the Game of Troy in Virgil's *Aeneid*. The maze design is similar to that of the labyrinth in the floor of Chartres Cathedral in France. There is a copy made in iron fitted in the floor of Alkborough Church porch and also a small coloured version in a window in the church.

A maze with a similar pattern to the Julian's Bower is at Wing, Leicestershire, at the side of a lane at the east end of the village. Cut into the turf, too, it is 13 m (40 ft) in diameter, with grass banks bout 30 cm (1 ft) high. It is medieval in origin and thought to

Photographs by Aerofilms Limited.

This is another Victorian maze, and is at Madresfield Court, in Worcestershire.

have religious importance at that time as a way of undertaking a penance.

At Saffron Walden, Essex, there is a turf maze cut in the shape of a circle with smaller circles at four points. It may have been made before Christianity came to Britain and was used in a pagan festivity. In 1699 15 shillings, then a lot of money, was spent in repairing it. Not too far away, at Hilton, Cambridgeshire, is a circular turf maze cut to a depth of 30 cm (1 ft) at the corner of the village green with 37 cm (15 in) wide paths and separating banks that lead to the centre. Here there is a tall pillar inscribed in Latin stating that it was set up by a William Sparrow in 1660 and the 'gyros' or paths were formed then, indicating that he paid for them to be recut and the maze restored. On top of the pillar is a ball sundial.

Mazes are still being created today, by landscape gardening companies for people with large gardens who want something different than usual garden ornaments of objects. One, called the Beatles Maze, to commemorate the famous Liverpool pop group, was built in 1984 for the Liverpool International Garden Festival and was visited by the Queen and Prince Philip when she opened the event on 2nd May that year.

If you would like to make a maze it is not too difficult. A fairly large flat open area is needed, such as a lawn or concreted pavement. For a permanent hedge maze an area of garden is required and small evergreen shrubs such as privet, box or yew.

If made on a lawn, sticks, all about the same length, are pushed into the turf to form the pattern. On a pavement bricks and parts of bricks would be ideal as they are flat and would form a wall as the maze sides, but if not obtainable fairly large, not too thin pieces of rock or stone, or even pebbles, can be used.

First draw the plan of the maze, with a least two entrances on each side, all leading to blind ends, except the one which leads to the centre. If you do not want to think up your own maze plan an alternative is to adapt one of the picture mazes published in *The Brownie*. Chalk can be used to draw the outlines of the paths, edges, entrances, etc on pavement or concrete, as it is not permanent and will wash off. On a lawn lay out the sticks flat on the grass in the required pattern, or you can use string attached to pegs pushed into the grass to form the maze outlines. Make the paths slightly wider than your own body width or at least double the width of your own two feet so that it will be possible to walk on the paths without touching the edges.

Now walk up and down the paths from the entrances to test them and make sure there is only one path leading to the centre. At the centre you could put some object, perhaps a garden gnome, or a bowl of water for birds. Another idea is to put a chair to rest on after walking up and down your maze. Even real mazes sometimes have seats in them so that visitors can sit down and get their breath back.

Having made sure the maze is correctly planned, place the rocks, stones or pebbles on the chalked lines, starting from the four outside edges of the square and working your way inwards to the centre. Similarly, if using a lawn, push the gathered sticks into the turf along the lines of the string at about the same height so they look level. The sticks do not have to be very close together. About 15 cm (6 in) apart will still form the maze.

When finished much fun can be had by asking your friends and relatives to try your maze. Admission of a few pence could be charged to do so, the collected money being given to local Brownie funds or your favourite charity.

Plan for a maze made with rocks and pebbles.

COMPETITION

WIN A CAMERA

Even though it may be Christmas time when you read this, I'm sure you will be able to remember the fun you had during the Summer, on holiday with your family, or perhaps with your Brownie Pack.

For this year's competition, I'd like you to paint or draw a picture, or write a report or story about your holiday. On the back of your entry, please clearly print your name, address, age and Brownie Pack. Also, please list the three items you liked best in this Annual. This will help to make the next Annual better still!

Send your entry to:

The Editor,
The Brownie Annual,
The Girl Guides Association,
17–19 Buckingham Palace Road,
London SW1W 0PT

The closing date for entries is 31 March 1986, and the winner will be notified by post. The editor's decision is final.

Puzzle answers

WORD SQUARE (page 24)

1. Good Turn
2. Gnome
3. Uniform
4. Olave
5. First Aid
6. Baden-Powell
7. Footpath
8. Trefoil
9. Note
10. Six
11. Highway
12. Imp
13. Flag
14. Road
15. Interest
16. Elf
17. Home
18. Lend a Hand
19. Pow-wow
20. Maps
21. Pack
22. Stop
23. Cook
24. Pool
25. Toy
26. Dive
27. Oak
28. Fun
29. Camp
30. Sing
31. Knot
32. Knit
33. Sixer
34. Bed

JUMBLED TOWNS (page 24)
The eighth town is KESWICK

BADGE SYMBOLS (page 29)

1. Frog
2. Panda
3. Magnifying Glass
4. Ark
5. Saucepan
6. Arrow
7. Wool
8. Cat
9. Web
10. Dancer

A	S	A	U	W	O	A	D	I	S
M	A	G	N	I	F	Y	I	N	G
A	U	B	A	N	T	E	R	G	L
S	C	A	R	R	O	W	O	T	A
T	E	E	R	E	A	R	T	I	S
A	P	I	O	P	F	R	I	N	S
D	A	N	C	E	R	C	W	E	B
S	N	E	F	O	A	E	K	C	E
W	D	O	D	T	M	A	R	A	W
A	A	B	W	O	O	L	A	M	S

Spot the Herb:(page 29)
1: Sage 2: Rosemary 3: Parsley 4: Mint
5: Basil 6: Camomile
7: Lavender 8: Liquorice

WORK IT OUT (page 29)
Sally had 48p; Lucy had 30p

Maze Game

illustrated by Tony Rose